A Sympathy of Souls

A Sympathy of Souls

ESSAYS BY ALBERT GOLDBARTH

COFFEE HOUSE PRESS :: MINNEAPOLIS :: 1990

These eight essays have previously appeared in journals as follows: "Wind-Up Sushi" in *The Denver Quarterly;* "After Yitzl," "Parade March from 'That Creaturely World,'" and "The Space" in *The Georgia Review;* "Ellen's," and "Fuller" in *The Kenyon Review;* "Threshold" in *New England Review/Bread Loaf Quarterly;* and "Calling Up" in *The New Virginia Review.*

"After Yitzl" was included in the 1988 editions of *The Pushcart Prize: The Best of the Small Presses* and *The Best American Essays;* "Parade March from 'That Creaturely World'" was included in the 1989 edition of *The Best American Essays.*

A Guggenheim Fellowship and a Fellowship from the National Endowment for the Arts enabled the completion of some of these pieces; the author expresses his gratitude to the sponsoring organizations.

Cover illustration by Susan Nees.
Back cover photo by Skyler Lovelace.

The publisher thanks the following organizations whose support helped make this book possible: The National Endowment for the Arts, a federal agency; Dayton Hudson Foundation; Cowles Media/ Star Tribune; Northwest Area Foundation; and United Arts.

Coffee House Press books are distributed to trade by CONSORTIUM BOOK SALES AND DISTRIBUTION, 287 East Sixth Street, Suite 365, Saint Paul, Minnesota 55101. Our books are also available through all major library distributors and jobbers, and through most small press distributors, including Bookpeople, Bookslinger, Inland, Pacific Pipeline, and Small Press Distribution. For personal orders, catalogs or other information, write to:
COFFEE HOUSE PRESS
27 NORTH FOURTH STREET, SUITE 400, MINNEAPOLIS, MN 55401.

Library of Congress Cataloging in Publication Data
Goldbarth, Albert.
A sympathy of souls : essays / by Albert Goldbarth.
These essays have previously appeared in various journals.
Contents: After Yitzl–Parade march from "That creaturely world" –Fuller–Threshold–Wind-up Sushi–Ellen's–Calling Up–The Space.
ISBN 0-918273-77-3 : $9.95
I. Title.
PS3557.0354S9 1990 90-31254
814'.54—DC20 CIP

Contents

for Skyler

Note

These pieces have been written over a decade. In ten years the names of the people in one's life will vary, small fillips of style will change, a few motifs and turns of phrase will repeat. While these pieces are not collected in chronological order of composition, no attempt has been made to alter the texts themselves toward an artificial after-the-fact consistency.

"This is a relation that will beget some wonder, and it well may; for most of our world are at present possessed with an opinion that visions and miracles are ceased. And, though it is most certain that two lutes, being both strung and tuned to an equal pitch, and then one played upon, the other that is not touched, being laid upon a table at a fit distance, will — like an echo to a trumpet — warble a faint audible harmony in answer to the same tune; yet many will not believe there is any such thing as a sympathy of souls; and I am well pleased that every reader do enjoy his own opinion."

— Izaak Walton

After Yitzl

> It is not for nothing that a Soviet historian once remarked that the most difficult of a historian's tasks is to predict the past.
>
> — Bernard Lewis, *History*

I.

This story begins in bed, in one of those sleepy troughs between the crests of sex. I stroke the crests of you. The night is a gray permissive color.

"Who do you think you were—do you think you were anyone, in an earlier life?"

In an earlier life, I think, though chance and bombs and the saltgrain teeth in ocean air have destroyed all documents, I farmed black bent-backed turnips in the hardpan of a shtetl compound of equally black-garbed bent-backed grandmama and rabbinic Jews.

My best friend there shoed horses. He had ribs like barrel staves, his sweat was miniature glass pears. (I'm enjoying this now.) On Saturday nights, when the Sabbath was folded back with its pristine linens into drawers for another week, this Yitzl played accordion at the schnapps-house. He was in love with a woman, a counter girl, there. She kept to herself. She folded paper roses in between serving; she never looked up. But Yitzl could tell: she tapped her foot. One day the cousin from Milano, who sent the accordion, sent new music to play—a little sheaf with American writing on it. *Hot* polka. Yitzl took a break with me in the corner—I was sipping sweet wine as dark as my turnips and trying to write a poem—and when he returned to his little grocer's crate of a stand, there was an open paper rose on his accordion. So he knew, then.

In this story-*in*-my-story they say "I love you," and now I say it in the external story, too: I stroke you slightly rougher as I say it, as if underlining the words, or reaffirming you're here, and I'm here, since the gray in the air is darker, and sight insufficient. You murmur it back. We say it like anyone else—in part because our death is bonded into us meiotically, from before there was marrow or myelin, and we know it, even as infants our scream is for more than the teat. We understand the wood smoke in a tree is aching to rise from the tree in its shape, its green and nutritive damps are readying always for joining the ether around it—any affirming clench of the roots in soil, physical and deeper, is preventive for its partial inch of a while.

So: genealogy. The family tree. Its roots. Its urgent suckings among the cemeterial layers. The backsweep of teat under teat. The way, once known, it orders the Present. A chief on the island of Nios, off Sumatra, could stand in the kerosene light of his plank hut and (this is on tape) recite—in a chant, the names sung out between his betel-reddened teeth like ghosts still shackled by hazy responsibility to the living—his ancestral linkup, seventy generations deep; it took over an hour. The genealogical record banks of the Mormon Church contain the names and relationship data of 1 1/2 to 2 billion of the planet's dead, "in a climate-controlled and nuclear-bomb-proof repository" called Granite Mountain Vault, and these have been processed through the Church's IBM computer system, the Genealogical Information and Names Tabulation, acronymed GIANT.

Where we come from. How we need to know.

If necessary, we'll steal it—those dinosaur tracks two men removed from the bed of Cub Creek in Hays County, using a masonry saw, a jackhammer, and a truck disguised as an ice cream vendor's.

If necessary (two years after Yitzl died, I married his schnapps-house sweetie: it was mourning him that initially drew us together; and later, the intimacy of hiding from the Secret Police in the burlap-draped back corner of a fishmonger's van. The guts were heaped to our ankles and our first true sex in there, as we rattled like bagged bones over the countryside, was lubricated—for fear kept her dry—with fishes' slime: and, after . . . but that's another story) we'll make it up.

2.

Which is what we did with love, you and I: invented it. We needed it, it wasn't here, and out of nothing in common we hammered a treehouse into the vee of a family tree, from zero, bogus planks, the bright but invisible nailheads of pure will. Some nights a passerby might spy us, while I was lazily flicking your nipple awake with my tongue, or you were fondling me into alertness, pleased in what we called bed, by the hue of an apricot moon, in what we called our life, by TV's dry-blue arctic light, two black silhouettes communing: and we were suspended in air. If the passerby yelled, we'd plummet.

Because each midnight the shears on the clock snip off another twenty-four hours. We're frightened, and rightfully so. Because glass is, we now know, a "slow liquid"; and we're slow dust. I've heard the universe howling—a conch from the beach is proof, but there are Ears Above for which the spiral nebulae must twist the same harrowing sound. Because pain, in even one cell, is an ant: it will bear a whole organ away. And a day is so huge—a Goliath; the tiny stones our eyes pick up in sleeping aren't enough to confront it. The marrow gives up. We have a spine, like a book's, and are also on loan with a due date. And the night is even more huge; what we call a day is only one struck match in an infinite darkness. This is knowledge we're born with, this is in the first cry. I've seen each friend I have, at one time or another, shake at thinking how susceptible and brief a person is: and whatever touching we do, whatever small narrative starring ourselves can bridge that unit of emptiness, is a triumph. "Tell me another story," you say with a yawn, "of life back then, with—what was her name?" "With Misheleh?" "Yes, with Misheleh." As if I can marry us backwards in time that way. As if it makes our own invented love more durable.

The Mormons marry backwards. "Sealing," they call it. In the sanctum of the temple, with permission called a "temple recommend," a Mormon of pious state may bind somebody long dead (perhaps an ancestor of his own, perhaps a name provided by chance from a list of cleared names in the computer)—bind that person to the Mormon faith, and to the flow of Mormon generations, in a retroactive conversion good "for time and all eternity." (Though the dead, they add, have "free agency" up in Heaven to accept this or not.) A husband and wife might be "celestially married" this way, from out of their graves and into the spun-sugar clouds of a Mormon Foreverness . . . from out of the Old World sod . . . from sand, from swampwater . . . Where does ancestry *stop?*

To pattern the present we'll fabricate the past from before there *was* fabric. Piltdown Man. On display in the British Museum. From 65 million years back—and later shown to be some forgery of human and orangutan lockings, the jawbone stained and abraded. Or, more openly and jubilant, the Civilization of Llhuros "from the recent excavations of Vanibo, Houndee, Draikum, and other sites"— in Ithaca, New York, Norman Daly, professor of art at Cornell and current "Director of Llhurosian Studies" has birthed an entire culture: its creatures (the Pruii bird, described in the article "Miticides of Coastal Llhuros"), its rites (". . . the Tokens of Holmeek are lowered into the Sacred Fires, and burned with the month-cloths of the Holy Whores"), its plaques and weapons and votive figurines, its myths and water clocks, its poems and urns and a "nasal flute." An elephant mask. An "early icon of Tal-Hax." Wall paintings. "Oxen bells." Maps. The catalogue I have is 48 pages—135 entries. Some of the Llhuros artifacts are paintings or sculpture. Some are anachronismed, a five-and-dime on-sale orange juicer becomes a *trallib,* an "oil container . . . Middle Period, found at Draikum." A clothes iron: "Late Archaic . . . that it may be a votive of the anchorite Ur Ur cannot be disregarded." Famous athletes. Textiles. "Fornicating gods."

Just open the mind, and the past it requires will surface. "Psychic archaeologists" have tranced themselves to the living worlds of the pyramids or the caves — one chipped flint scraper can be connection enough. When Edgar Cayce closed his eyes he opened them (inside his head, which had its eyes closed) in the undiluted afternoon light of dynastic Egypt: wind was playing a chafing song in the leaves of the palm and the persea, fishers were casting their nets. "His findings and methods tend to be dismissed by the orthodox scientific community," but Jeffrey Goodman meditates, and something — an invisible terraform diving bell of sorts — descends with his eyes to fully twenty feet below the sands of Flagstaff, Arizona, 100,000 B.C., his vision brailling happily as a mole's nose through the bones set in the darkness there like accent marks and commas.

Going back . . . The darkness . . . Closing your lids . . .

A wheel shocked into a pothole. Misheleh waking up, wild-eyed. Torches.

"We needed certain papers, proof that we were Jews, to be admitted to America. To pass the inspectors there. And yet if our van was stopped by the Secret Police and we were discovered in back, those papers would be our death warrant. Such a goat's dessert! — that's the expression we used then."

"And . . . ?"

"It comes from when two goats will fight for the same sweet morsel — each pulls a different direction."

"No, I mean that night, the escape — what *happened?*"

"The Secret Police stopped the van."

3.

Earlier, I said "in a trough between crests" — sea imagery. I mean in part that dark, as it grows deeper, takes the world away, and a sleepless body will float all night in horrible separation from what it knows and where it's nurtured. Freedom is sweet; but nobody wants to be flotsam.

Ruth Norman, the eighty-two-year-old widow of Ernest L. Norman, is Uriel, an Archangel, to her fellow Unarian members and is, in fact, the "Cosmic Generator," and head of all Unarius activities on Earth (which is an applicant for the "Intergalactic Confederation" of thirty-two other planets—but we need to pass a global test of "consciousness vibration"). In past lives, Uriel has been Socrates, Confucius, Henry VIII, and Benjamin Franklin—and has adventured on Vidus, Janus, Vulna, and other planets. All Unarians know their former lives. Vaughn Spaegel has been Charlemagne. And Ernest L. himself has been Jesus (as proved by a pamphlet, *The Little Red Box*) and currently is Alta; from his ankh-shaped chair on Mars he communicates psychically and through a bank of jeweled buttons with all the Confederation. Everyone works toward the day Earth can join. The 1981 Conclave of Light, at the Town and Country Convention Center in El Cajon, California, attracted over 400 Unarians, some from as far as New York and Toronto. Neosha Mandragos, formerly a nun for twenty-seven years, was there; and George, the shoestore clerk, and Dan, assistant manager of an ice cream parlor.

Uriel makes her long-awaited entrance following the *Bolero*-backed procession of two girls dressed as peacocks, led by golden chains, then two nymphs scattering petals from cornucopias, someone wearing a feathered bird's head, and various sages. Four "Nubian slaves . . . wearing skin bronzer, headdresses, loincloths and gilded beach thongs" carry a palanquin adorned with enormous white swans, atop which . . . Uriel! In a black velvet gown falling eight feet wide at the hem, with a wired-up universe of painted rubber balls representing the thirty-two worlds and dangling out to her skirt's edge. According to Douglas Curran, "the gown, the painted golden 'vortex' headdress, and the translucent elbow-length gloves with rapier nails have tiny light bulbs snaked through the fabric. The bulbs explode into volleys of winking. Waves of light roll from bodice to fingertips, Infinite Mind to planets." People weep. Their rich remembered lives are a sudden brilliance over their nerves, like ambulance flashers on chicken wire, like . . . like fire approaching divinity. Nobody's worrying here over last week's sales of butter-pecan parfait.

We'll sham it. We need it. It's not that we lie. It's that we *make* the truth. The Japanese have a word especially for it: *nisekeizu,* false genealogies. Ruling-class Japan was obsessed with lineage and descent, and these connived links to the Sewangezi line of the Fujiwaras qualified one—were indeed the only qualification at the time—for holding office. "High birth." "Pedigree." It's no less likely in Europe. In the seventeenth century, Countess Alexandrine von Taxis "hired genealogists to fabricate a descent from the Torriani, a clan of warriors who ruled Lombardy until 1311."

European Jews, who by late in the 1700s needed to take on surnames in order to cross a national border, often invented family names that spoke of lush green woods and open fields—this from a people traipsing from one cramped dingy urban ghetto to another. Greenblatt. Tannenbaum. Now a child born choking on soot could be heir to a name saying miles of mild air across meadows. Flowers. Mossy knolls.

Misheleh's name was Rosenblum. I never asked but always imagined this explained the trail of paper roses she'd left through Yitzl's life. My name then was Schvartzeit, reference to my many-thousand-year heritage of black beets. The name on our papers, though, was Kaufman—"merchant." This is what you had to do, to survive.

I remember: they were rough with us, also with the driver of the van. But we pretended being offended, like any good citizens. It could have gone worse. This was luckily early in the times of the atrocities, and these officers—they were hounds set out to kill, but they went by the book. A hound is honest in his pursuit. The rat and the slippery eel—later on, more officers were like that.

They might have dragged us away just for being in back of the van at all. But we said we were workers. In this, the driver backed us up. And the papers that shouted out *Jew?* My Misheleh stuffed them up a salmon. Later, after the Secret Police were gone and we had clumped across the border, we were on our knees with a child's doll's knife slicing the bellies of maybe a hundred fish until we found it! Covered in pearly offal and roe. We had it framed when we came to America. Pretty. A little cherrywood frame with cherubim puffing a trump in each corner. We were happy, then. A very lovely frame around an ugliness.

"And you loved each other."

Every day, in our hearts. Some nights, in our bodies. I'll tell you this about sex: it's like genealogy. Yes. It takes you back, to the source. That's one small bit of why some people relish wallowing there. A burrowing, completely and beastly, back to where we came from. It tastes and smells "fishy" in every language I know. It takes us down to when the blood was the ocean, down the rivers of the live flesh to the ocean, to the original beating fecundity. It's as close as we'll ever get.

And this I'll tell you, about the smell of fish: For our earliest years, when I was starting the dry goods store and worrying every bolt of gabardine or every bucket of nails was eating another poem out of my soul — which I think is true — we lived over a fish store. Kipper, flounder, herring, the odors reached up like great gray leaves through our floorboards. And every night we lived there, Misheleh cried for a while. After the van, you see? She could never be around raw fish again, without panic.

But on the whole we were happy. There was security of a kind, and friends — even a social club in a patchy back room near the train tracks, that we decorated once a month with red and yellow crepe festoons and paper lanterns pouring out a buttery light.

Once every year she and I, we visited the cemetery. A private ritual: we pretended Yitzl was buried there. Because he'd brought us together, and we wanted him with us yet. For the hour it took, we always hired a street accordionist — it wasn't an uncommon instrument then. Like guitar now. Play a polka, we told him — *hot*. It drove the other cemetery visitors crazy! And always, Misheleh left a paper rose at the cemetery gates.

We heard that accordion music and a whole world came back, already better and worse than it was in its own time. Harsher. Gentler. Coarser. Little things — our shtetl dogs. Or big things too, the way we floated our sins away on toy-sized cork rafts once each spring, and everybody walking home singing . . . All of that world was keeping its shape but growing more and more transparent for us. Like the glass slipper in the fairy tale. The past was becoming a fairy tale. In it, the slipper predicates a certain foot and, so, a certain future.

At night I'd walk in my store. The moon like a dew on the barrel heaped with bolts, and the milky bodies of lamps, and the pen nibs, and shovels . . . Kaufman. Merchant.

4.

Within a year after death we have what Jewish tradition calls "the unveiling"—the gravestone dedication ceremony. September 14, 1986: I arrived in Chicago, joining my mother, sister, two aunts, and perhaps thirty others, including the rabbi, at the grave of my father Irving Goldbarth, his stone wrapped in a foolish square of cheesecloth. A stingy fringe of grass around the fresh mound. The burial had taken place in bitter city winter, the earth (in my memory) opening with the crack of axed oak. Now it was warmer, blurrier, everything soft. My mother's tears.

The rabbi spoke, his voice soft: to the Jews a cemetery is "a house of graves" . . . but also a "house of eternal life." The same in other faiths, I thought. There are as many dead now as alive. A kind of balance along the ground's two sides. That permeable membrane. Always new dead in the making, and always the long dead reappearing over our shoulders and in our dreams. Sometimes a face, like a coin rubbed nearly smooth, in a photo. We're supposed to be afraid of ghosts but every culture has them, conjures them, won't let go. Our smoky ropes of attachment to the past. Our anti-umbilici . . . My mind wandering. Then, the eldest and only son, I'm reciting the Kaddish. "Yisgadahl v'yisgadosh sh'may rahbbo . . ." In back, my father's father's grave, the man I'm named for. Staring hard and lost at the chiseling, ALBERT GOLDBARTH. My name. His dates.

In 1893 "Albert Goldbarth An Alien personally appeared in open Court and prayed to be admitted to become a Citizen of the United States . . ."—I have that paper, that and a sad, saved handful of others: September 15, 1904, he "attained the third degree" in the "Treue Bruder Lodge of the Independent Order of Odd Fellows." Five days after, J. B. Johnson, General Sales

Agent of the Southern Cotton Oil Company, wrote a letter recommending "Mr. Goldbarth to whomsoever he may apply, as an honest and hardworking Salesman, leaving us of his own accord." That was 24 Broad Street, New York. In two years, in Cleveland, Ohio, John H. Silliman, Secretary, was signing a notice certifying Mr. Albert Goldbarth as an agent of The American Accident Insurance Company. And, from 1924, "$55 Dollars, in hand paid," purchasing Lot Number 703 – this, from the envelope he labeled in pencil "Paid Deed from Semetery Lot from Hibrew Progresif Benefit Sociaty." I'm standing there now. I'm reading this stone that's the absolute last of his documents.

There aren't many stories. Just two photographs. And he was dead before I was born. A hundred times, I've tried inventing the callouses, small betrayals, tasseled mantle lamps, day-shaping waves of anger, flicked switches, impossible givings of love in the face of no love, dirty jokes, shirked burdens, flowerpots, loyalties, gold-shot silk page markers for the family Bible, violin strings, sweet body stinks from the creases, knickknacks, lees of tea, and morning-alchemized trolley tracks declaring themselves as bright script in the sooted-over paving bricks – everything that makes a life, which is his life, and buried.

And why am I busy repeating that fantastical list . . .? We're "mountain gorillas" (this is from Alex Shoumatoff's wonderful study of kinship, *The Mountain of Names*) who "drag around moribund members of their troop and try to get them to stand, and after they have died" (above my grandfather's grave, imagining bouts of passion with imaginary Misheleh over my grandfather's grave now) "masturbate on them and try to get some reaction from them." An offering, maybe. A trying to read life backwards into that text of dead tongues. Give us any fabric scrap, we'll dream the prayer shawl it came from. Give us any worthless handful of excavated soil, we'll dream the scrap. The prayer. The loom the shawl took fragile shape on, in the setting shtetl hill-light. The immigrant ships they arrived in, the port, the year. We'll give that year whatever version of semen is appropriate, in homage and resuscitative ritual. We'll breathe into, rub, and luster that year.

1641: On a journey in Ecuador, a Portuguese Jew, Antonio de Montezinos, discovered – after a week-long, brush-clogged hell trek through the hinterlands—a hidden Jewish colony, and heard them wailing holy writ in Hebrew. Yes, there in the wild domain of anaconda and peccary—or so he told the Jewish scholar and eminent friend of Rembrandt, Menasseh ben Israel. Or so Menasseh claimed, who had his own damn savvy purposes; and based on his claim that the Ten Lost Tribes of Israel were now found in the New World, and their global equi-dispersion near complete—as the Bible foretells will usher in an Age of Salvation—Britain's Puritan leaders readmitted their country's exiled Jews, the better to speed the whole world on its prophesied way to Redemption. (Maybe Rembrandt was an earlier body of Ernest L. Norman? Maybe the massed Confederation planets were holding their astro-collective breath even then, as destiny wound like spool thread on the windmills. And maybe, in the same Dutch-sunset oranges and mauves he let collect like puddled honey in his painted-dusk skies, Rembrandt helped Menasseh finagle this plot on behalf of a troubled people, tipped a flagon of burgundy in a room of laundered varnish rags, and plotted as the radio-telescope Monitor Maids of planet Vidus lounged about in their gold lamé uniforms, listening . . .)

Maybe. Always a maybe. Always someone forcing the scattered timbers of history into a sensible bridge. The Lost Tribes: China. The Lost Tribes: Egypt. The Lost Tribes: Africa. India. Japan. They formed a kingdom near "a terrible river of crashing stones" that roared six days a week "but on the Jewish Sabbath did cease." Lord Kingsborough emptied the family fortune, won three stays in debtor's prison, "in order to publish a series of sumptuously illustrated volumes proving the Mexican Indians . . ." Ethiopians. Eskimos. The Mormons have them reaching America's shores as early as "Tower of Babylon times" and later again, about 600 B.C., becoming tipi dwellers, hunters of lynx and buffalo, children of Fire and Water Spirits . . . Maybe. But today I think these caskets in Chicago soil are voyage enough. The moon's not that far.

We visit the other family graves: Auntie Regina (brain cancer) . . . Uncle Jake (drank; slipped me butterscotch candies) . . . Miles square and unguessably old, this cemetery's a city, districted, netted by streets and their side roads, overpopulated, undercared. Dead Jews dead Jews dead Jews. *Ruth Dale Noparstak * Age 2 Weeks * 1944*—death about the size of a cigar box.

My mother says to Aunt Sally (a stage whisper): "You'll see, Albert's going to write a poem about this." Later, trying to help that endeavor: "Albert, you see these stones on the graves? Jews leave stones on the graves to show they've visited." Not flowers? Why not flowers? . . . *I think I farmed black bent-backed turnips in the hardpan of a shtetl compound of equally black-garbed bent-backed grandmama and rabbinic Jews.*

My mother's parents are here in the Moghileff section, "Organized 1901." "You see the people here? They came from a town called Moghileff, in Russia—or it was a village. Sally, was Moghileff a town or a village?—you know, a little place where all the Jews lived. And those who came to Chicago, when they died, they were all buried here. Right next to your Grandma and Grandpa's graves, you see?—Dave and Natalie?—they were Grandma and Grandpa's neighbors in Moghileff, and they promised each other that they'd stay neighbors forever, here."

"Your Grandma Rosie belonged to the Moghileff Sisterhood. She was Chairlady of Relief. That meant, when somebody had a stillbirth, or was out of a job, or was beat in an alley, she'd go around to the members with an empty can and collect five dollars." Sobbing now. "Five dollars."

On our way out there's a lavish mausoleum lording it over this ghetto of small gray tenanted stones. My Uncle Lou says, still in his Yiddish-flecked English: "And *dis* one?" Pauses. "Gotta be a gengster."

5.

The Mormons marry backwards. "Sealing," they call it.

"Is that the end of your story of Misheleh and you?"

The story of marrying backwards never ends.

In Singapore not long ago, the parents of a Miss Cheeh, who had been stillborn twenty-seven years before, were troubled by ghosts in their dreams, and consulted a spirit medium. Independently, the parents of a Mr. Poon consulted her too—their son had been stillborn thirty-six years earlier and, recently, ghosts were waking them out of slumber. "And the medium, diagnosing the two ghosts' problem as loneliness, acted as their marriage broker." The Poons and the Cheehs were introduced, a traditional bride price paid, and dolls representing the couple were fashioned out of paper, along with a miniature one-story house with manservant, car, and chauffeur, a table with teacups and pot, and a bed with bolster and pillows. Presumably, on some plane of invisible, viable, ectoplasmic endeavor, connubial bliss was enabled. Who knows?—one day soon, they may wake in their version of that paper bed (his arm around her sex-dampened nape, a knock at the door . . .) and be given the chance to be Mormon, to have always been Mormon, and everlastingly Mormon. They'll laugh, but graciously. She'll rise and start the tea . . .

These ghosts. Our smoky ropes of attachment. And our reeling them in.

Eventually Misheleh and I prospered. The store did well, then there were two stores. We grew fat on pickled herring in cream, and love. I suppose we looked jolly. Though you could see in the eyes, up close, there was a sadness: where our families died in the camps, where I was never able to find time for the poetry—those things. Even so, the days and nights were good. The children never lacked a sweet after meals (but only if they cleaned their plates), or a little sailor suit, or kewpie blouse, or whatever silliness was in fashion. Before bed, I'd tell them a story. *Once, your mother and I, we lived in another country. A friend introduced us. He was a famous musician. Your mother danced to his songs and a thousand people applauded. I wrote poems about her, everyone read them. Gentlemen flung her roses . . .*

I died. It happens. I died and I entered the Kingdom of Worm and of God, and what happens then isn't part of this story, there aren't any words for it. And what I became on Earth—here, in the memory of the living . . . ?—it isn't over yet, it never ends, and now I'm me and I love you.

Because the ash is in this paper in which I'm writing (and in the page you're reading) and has been from the start. Because the blood is almost the chemical composition of the ocean, the heart is a swimmer, a very sturdy swimmer, but shore is never in sight. Because of entropy. Because of the nightly news. Because the stars care even less for us than we do for the stars. Because the only feeling a bone can send us is pain. Because the more years that we have, the less we have — the schools don't teach this Tragic Math but we know it; twiddling the fingers is how we count it off. Because because because. And so somebody wakes from an ether sleep: the surgeons have made him Elvis, he can play third-rate Las Vegas bars. And so someone revises the raven on top of the clan pole to a salmon-bearing eagle: now his people have a totem-progenitor giving them certain territorial privileges that the spirits ordained on the First Day of Creation. So. Because.

In *He Done Her Wrong*, the "Great American Novel — in pictures — and not a word in it" that the brilliant cartoonist Milt Gross published in 1930, the stalwart square-jawed backwoods hero and his valiant corn-blonde sweetheart are torn from each other's arms by a dastardly mustachioed villain of oily glance and scowling brow, then seemingly endless deprivations begin: fistfights, impoverishment, unbearable loneliness, the crazed ride down a sawmill tied to one of its logs . . . And when they're reunited, as if that weren't enough, what cinches it as a happy ending is uncinched buckskin pants: the hero suddenly has a strawberry birthmark beaming from his tush, and is known for the billionaire sawmill owner's rightful heir . . .

Because it will save us.

The story-in-my-story is over: Misheleh and the children walk home from the cemetery. She's left a stone and a paper rose. We never would have understood it fifty years earlier, sweated with sex, but this is also love.

The story is over, too: the "I" is done talking, the "you" is nearly asleep, they lazily doodle each other's skin. We met them, it seems a long while ago, in what I called "a trough between crests." Let their bed be a raft, and let the currents of sleep be calm ones.

Outside of the story, I'm writing this sentence, and whether someone is a model for the "you" and waiting to see me put my pen down and toe to the bedroom — or even if I'm just lonely, between one "you" and the next — is none of your business. The "outside" is never the proper business between a writer and a reader, but this I'll tell you: tonight the rains strafed in, then quit, and the small symphonic saws of the crickets are swelling the night. This writing is almost over.

But nothing is ever over — or, if it is, then the impulse is wanting to *make* it over: "over" not as in "done," but "again." "Redo." Re-synapse. Re-nova.

I need to say "I love you" to someone and feel it flow down the root of her, through the raw minerals, over the lip of the falls, and back, without limit, into the pulse of the all-recombinant waters.

I meet Carolyn for lunch. She's with Edward, her old friend, who's been living in the heart of Mexico all of these years:

> Our maid, Rosalita, she must be over seventy. She had "female troubles," she said. She needed surgery. But listen: she's from the hills, some small collection of huts that doesn't even bear a name, so she hasn't any papers at all — absolutely no identification. There isn't a single professional clinic that can accept you that way. There isn't any means for obtaining insurance or public aid.
>
> So we went to a Records Division. I slipped the agent *dinero*. He knew what I was doing. It's everywhere. It's the way Mexico works. And when we left, Rosalita was somebody else. She had somebody else's birth certificate, working papers — everything.
>
> She had somebody else's life from the beginning, and she could go on with her own.

Author's Note: In the writing of this essay I drew on many rich sources of information and inspiration, two of which deserve special mention: Douglas Curran's *In Advance of the Landing: Folk Concepts of Outer Space* (1986) and Alex Shoumatoff's *The Mountain of Names: An Informal History of Kinship* (1985).

Parade March from *That Creaturely World*

The halved ham, with its dipsy smile and majorette boots. The headdress-topped pineapple in its sleek-lined 1950s bowl like a chieftain in canoe. The dapper pepper mill. The jitterbugging celery and tomato . . .

I would keep my father company on weekends. Mr. Penny-Insurance-Peddler. Mr. Schlep-and-Sell. He schmoozed, but he was honest. "Albie, you'll see. I'll joke but I won't lie." Mostly I didn't see, I stayed in the car while he labored up four floors with his enormously heavy leatherette case of waiting dotted lines, his promo giveaway cookbooks. I didn't want to go partners in this. 1956 — I was eight, I was only eight, but already it was clear to me: the fiscal wasn't my world.

So I sprawled dreamy on the front seat with the reading at hand. It was there in the car when we all went on vacation every summer, and it was in the apartment like water or electricity, some natural phenomenon you didn't question: *The Metropolitan Life Insurance Cook Book.* There were days, I suppose, when I spent more time in its heavily stylized cosmos — with those leapfrogging muffins, barbershop-quartet condiment bottles, deckle-edged lettuces, troupes of onion acrobats — than I did with my neighborhood friends.

"Memory food" my mother called fish. Is that why the shad on page eleven, his body so scaled it's artichoke-like, looks doleful? Would he like to forget? Carrots were "good for your eyes" — though even then, I think I sensed that these ridiculous penile guys moved through their proper earthy domain by touch alone. What stayed with me most accurately was the final parade at the top of page 60, a marching pie with a pennant, a pear who's pouring his full rotundity into a trumpet blast . . .

Once in a while I did go up. These were buildings scant blocks out of some ghetto, where a brief shot at a foreman's job meant cheap-pink-gingham-curtained windows that might have been simply newspapered one year back. These were families ready to think *insurance* — Greek, Italian, Polish versions of the Jewish home I'd waked in that morning. Walking up the hallway — always to something like "Apartment 4D" in a courtyard building done in the thirties, its bricks a liver color . . . The smells of other-ethnic simmers wooed and unsettled me. Moussaka. Duck-blood soup.

I remember now: Mrs. Poniewiecz didn't know how to say it, coughed politely, roved her eyes. And it was true: I was trying to leave with 40¢ of *her* polite negotiations in my fist. *He* was so flustered; there was no joke for this. He built a rococo architecture of foot-shuffle and apology, and I was ashamed: for him, not for myself. To me, it hadn't really seemed thieving. Just as those cartoon foods were my natural environment — not the intricate, ordinary grown-ups' world of the kitchen — so, too, the winking small change making its way through the riffle of tens of dollars was *my* province. Anyway, it only happened the once; I wasn't inveterate.

Oh, but I could feel, I could *hear,* him turning red with embarrassment. Maybe that's why, all these years, I'd "remembered" a crimson lobster topping one page, a lobster in some unexplained dismay, although when I chanced on the book last week at a flea market . . . there's no lobster at all.

* * * *

One of the luckless in the D.C. drug-trade wars, age twenty, was thrown in a motel bathtub filling with scalding water. This you don't forget: "As his skin was peeling off, they took turns urinating on him."

How ashamed would I have to feel for thinking *lobster,* for the tic that starts a joke from this scenario? But I did think that.

I read the story in *Time* that same afternoon I excavated the cookbook from its clutterbox of spotted farmer's almanacs and fifties "humor magazines" with teasing swimsuit cuties and titles like *Wink* and *Wow*.

He must have given out a terrible sound — even if it were silent, even if it only shrieked on the level of where his cellular chemistry broke, then altered.

Two texts, and I couldn't help think what I thought. It's night. I'm walking under stars we like to believe are stories or beam down influence over our lives, but how much here is ever seen in a nebulous "there"? I know the lettuce on three is frilled like a petticoated belle, the chickpea leaps arms out with cockamamie grace, the small soup-carrot rides its spoon as if some mermaid-costumed carnival queen in a Mardi Gras float . . .

And these two disparate texts and their denizens are real and both exist in the same world. This can't be but is.

And it can't be I wasn't there to hear that sound he made, I remember it so distinctly.

And the sound my father made in Chicago when I was in Texas: an egg, a very tiny egg, of pain. Just the size of one period out of that cookbook. First he centered it on his tongue, in 1985, in the Edgewater Hospital cardiac ward, then swallowed until it filled him.

Is this a recipe?

I can taste it.

* * * *

And I see now what I couldn't (maybe *looked at,* yes, but not with real *seeing*) in those lolling hours waiting for my father in the half-paid-for fedora-gray '48 Chevy: that some of the cookbook's normally up-tempo population exhibits . . . well, twistedness.

A bowl of whites is being whipped by one of those hand-held eggbeaters looking as spiked and aggressive as any medieval mace. Of course it's a humanoid bowl, with two google-eyes near its rim peeking fearfully upward, and two spidery arms, the spidery hands of which fidget. Its brains, essentially, are being violently frothed. Its cranium is open to the skies while this crude instrument of torture whirs erratic, turbid circles through its silky insides.

Who drew a thing like that? Who gave the world page 37's dearly ambulatory sardine can — yes, with arms and legs, its oval lid keyed open, so we see its brains are three individual chartreuse fishlings in heavy oil? Whoever he is or was, he made certain the human condition was emblemized within an adequate range, some touch of its uttermost limits, before he drew the rest of his festive comforting crew: a momma teapot gaily pouring into a row of progeny cups, a group of sausages horsing around like the guys in the locker room, a single blissful layer cake as corpulent and knowing as a buddha.

I grew up with these. Once, age thirty, I needed a word for a poem, some part a tractor drags, and tried describing it to Tony and Theo. "Draw it for us," Tony told me. It was natural, my tractor had these headlight eyes and a smiling mechanical snout. Theo laughed. But Tony, who knew me longer and better, shook his head and said to her, "No, it's not that funny. You don't understand: *he REALLY sees the world that way*."

That angered me so much it had to be right. And it delighted me as well, in a way. I felt I'd been true to that eight-year-old boy and his beat, breadwinner father. I can see them, tired, cross with each other, but bonded by being tired and cross, driving home through five o'clock Saturday traffic. There's no radio; the father sings some popular hit. He loves the boy, who he hopes will join in. The boy knows it and won't. It's a ritual — even this bonds them. Sweaty, lazy, they stop at a carhop shack, it might be Buns & Suds, and bask as well as they can in the feel of two giant root beers. Even the Chevy gets to bask, in the shade of the corrugated tin. It sighs, I hear it sigh, and it dips its overwrought grille to that shade and drinks deeply.

* * * *

". . . we give a chair arms, legs, a seat and a back, a cup has its lip / and a bottle its neck"—this from a poem by Marvin Bell. Yes, and a potato its eyes. The mandrake we give an entire human body; if you tugged one from the soil in the year of our Lord 1500 it might squeal deafeningly, an infant being murdered. Just ask anyone.

In Elizabeth Bishop's persona monologue "Crusoe in England," the rescued speaker, old now, "bored too," back in a realm of courtesies and teatime, considers the knife that for so many years was his closest companion and (even following Friday's arrival) the fondled, talked-to, slept-with, absolutely unrelinquishable, major-causal object of his universe. It's a souvenir now. "The living soul has dribbled away."

That knife. The simple Mesopotamian oracle plate that held the watchful consciousness of a god in its glaze. Some thumb-long balsa doll a child has loved so nuzzlingly much the face is rubbed away inversely to the personality quickened inside it: "my Wubsie" (though why *Wubsie*, no one knows), you swear if you slipped that doll from her sleeping grip it would squeal like an infant being murdered . . .

These come from what David Jones calls, in the preface to his novel *In Parenthesis,* "that creaturely world inherited from our remote beginnings." He wonders (this in 1937) if we'll come to see "newfangled technicalities as true extensions of ourselves, that we may feel for them a native affection." Maybe. Ten years after, men were tightening the last of the nuts of the Chevy they'd premiere that fall and my father would buy a year later, and curse, and coddle-coo, and intimately discourse with, in ways I wouldn't have with any woman for a long bleak while, not even a woman I'd claim I "loved."

And I've watched my father's mother hold such forthright conversation with her ancient foot-treadle sewing machine. The bobbin was all business, but, oh, the vines carved over the wooden side-drawers on the body were like a factory worker's secret descending tattoos. She didn't know I was there. She stitched all night alone with it, and while I only heard *her* voice—a kind of singing, really—I have no reason to say a kind of dialogue wasn't taking place.

I've seen her sing to the soup, low and Yiddish-guttural, seen her sing to the chicken she disemboweled, until the face of the man I was named for must have risen visibly in the soup steam for her. What came then was the everyday talking of woman to man. He was dead. She was holding the heart of a chicken. Now I know, thirty-two years later: if she whistled, an ancient Egyptian bowl would arrive to receive that slick purple thing, would walk in slightly tilted on its own two childlike feet.

* * * *

The fries in their wire fryer, like goldfinches sleeking about a cage. The froufrou cabbage in her indigo chanteuse ruffles. All those frolicking Cub-Scout olives, deviled eggs, radish rosettes: the Appetizer Troop, out on maneuvers . . .

In the sixteenth century, somebody's grabbing a mandrake's gnarly top and yanking hard (her ears are beeswaxed closed to muffle its shrill of agony) . . . Somebody's curing a headache by smearing his scalp with a lard-based walnut paste; why? simple: the meat of the nut resembles the brain . . . "Matter," Morris Berman says in *The Reenchantment of the World,* "possessed consciousness." And then goes on, after detailing much of alchemical versus Newtonian cosmologies, to a "conclusion . . . that will probably strike most readers as radical in the extreme. . . . It is not merely the case that men conceived of matter as possessing mind in those days, but rather that in those days, matter *did* possess mind, 'actually' did so."

When I was eight, wedges of cheese ran races around the fondue tureen, a Spanish onion promenaded hand-in-hand with a steak sauce bottle whose black cap fit him snug as a derby . . .

Morris Berman: "The animism implicit in quantum mechanics has been explored mathematically by the physicist Evan Harris Walker, who argues that every particle in the universe possesses consciousness."

. . . the cherry tomato, sighing with love for the urbane, professorly roast.

And if they *are* a denatured version of such primacy? Still, they're a version.

* * * *

Skyler and Babs collect lobsterania: ashtrays, serving platters, blotters, squeeze toys, stamps, you name it.

What a creature! From the major bones of dinosaur, or of Cro-Magnon man, we can, in a rational process of retro-extrapolation, construct the whole. But who could guess *this* whisker-sprouting jointed castanet armory from its insides? When we eat one, overblooming its shell like a split couch pillow — all those buttersweet meat-feathers!

Lobster postcards are a specialty subgenre of postcard collecting. One, in high demand, is a photograph of The Lobsterettes: a chorine line in life-sized lobster costumes.

In a "fifties shop" in Kansas City, Skyler and I found a set of lobster salt-and-pepper shakers. They're standing up and might be rhumba partners or pugilists. Rarefied kitsch. They were screamingly fireplug-red on a shelf of pastel celadon and eggshell 1950s radios, whose round contours and unashamed dials and gawking or grinning station-bands easily give them the spirit of human faces.

In an African market, Skyler and Bobby Sue picked two apiece from wooden buckets and lugged them home by their antennae, giant specimens, a foot and a half. "They were lovely in their buckets — so many greens! They were . . . *hazel*." "Like eyes?" I ask her. "Yes, that many colors. Like hazel eyes."

Wasn't it Gérard de Nerval — some Symbolist poet — who in a fit of revel or breakdown walked a lobster on a leash?

And why am I doing this, talking around it? Here, let me say his name: *Patrick Monfiston*. Twenty years old, his skin heated past being skin, and the live piss eating him.

Babs owns an inflatable lobster and one that leaps when you press a small rubber bulb.

I know how comic they can be.

I know what salt means too. I can't play with that shaker and not hear contents shifting — even if the shaker's empty.

Every year at the Passover holiday, Jews dip a token of what they're feasting on into a basin of saltwater. To remind them of suffering. Wine and honey and singing until the table is cleared. And that: to remind them of suffering.

* * * *

I remember it this vividly: the dining-room light of that small apartment breaking into splinters on the knobules of the Kaddish goblet. Passover, and my father conducting the ceremonial meal. Grandma Nettie (yes, alive then) with her hands still bright from the only emollient they ever knew, fresh chicken fat. Uncle Morrie (alive then) making subterfuge cracker boats in his soup while the service drones on around us in Hebrew—he winks at me, but slyly. My mother. Aunt Sally. My sister Livia. The carpet is the sickly color of moss from a tree's wrong side, and Cousin Beverly's overenthusiastic oil portrait of Tuffy the poodle is still on the wall. And my father is singing the High Tongue, my father is opening Time itself until the days of the Bible pull chairs up to the table, and goatstink and angel shadows attend us. My father, alive then. I remember: his voice a ladder to God.

I remember, he demystified the intricacy of a necktie. I remember, once, in search of some keys I lucked upon the girlie coin ("heads"/"tails") under his handkerchiefs—that ripe clef of the body thereon. I remember his passion for home-pickling cukes. I remember his arm when he slammed on the brakes of the Chevy, instinctively bolting me safe from the windshield—do I really see it? Every hair, the cuff the day's stained gray.

And I can hear each lousy penny of that forty—one for each year of my life now—dropping out of my fingers, down the Grand Canyon, measured by Galileo himself for velocity, hitting the tin plate at the centermost magma of Earth and melting there to forty damp grains of salt.

I remember because I found them, in their camouflage of yellowed gazettes and palmistry tracts, and they're bringing it with them, all of it, and all of them, parading: the various eggs in their top hats and bonnets are here, and the drum-beating gourd, and the bread with his slices inching him along like the ribs of a snake, and the goof-off kidney and lima and chili beans like Shriners and Masons and lodge brothers everywhere marching and cavorting, and the burger gals are here, and the pear, and the phalanx of clown-nosed cookies . . .

And my dear old friend, the melancholy fish of page 11, isn't eaten.

Of course. Mr. Memory Food. Mr. Memory Food. Over time he'll consume himself.

Fuller

I.

She worked with burnt hands. Burnt, in a way, from the inside out. The tips were fine-cracked like old paintings. And she'd been working today, again, from even before the first blood-colored light of dawn rode along the hosed slops of the market gutters. Now, hours later, the air in the shed, gassy from the cauldrons, swelled the delicate skin inside the nose, was furry on her shoulders like a stole. And so she lay her face on the pine-wood table, resting in its inevitable coating of coal dust and iron grit . . .

The dream was the same, although — well, *thinner* this time, since she wasn't fully asleep. But it was the meteor all right. It flared across the darkness in her head, a lovely thing of tons, that was giving itself away by turning to light, until only a thimbleful remained.

That last irreducible splat of metal landed somewhere out of seeing. Some people — a few, and she was one — began a desperate search, devoting themselves completely to its finding: a flurried dream-montage of shovels, steam-powered digging contraptions, fever-dampened brows.

But at the same time as she was concentrating wholly on the earth-bound search, her dream-self saw that the light stayed on, a bright thing with a clear form, in the otherwise flat black sky. It was a giant flame, a kind of Bunsen burner flame with its recognizable spearhead shape, but then that seemed to break, reform, and take on a nimbus: more like the flame at an altar, in front of the niche where a totem spirit looked down . . .

It billowed—the nimbus, undoing itself like radiant veils fanned out from a dancer's hips. The flame was a lily. It blossomed, fragile, gold-white . . . It was butterfly wings. It was butterfly wings. *Flame and lily and butterfly wings . . .*

And then, as always, Marie Sklodowska Curie woke, reaching for the condenser plates, syringes, and electrometer.

The shed they called their lab was just that—an abandoned shed in the yard of the School of Physics and Chemistry, 42 Rue Lhomond. Its glass roof couldn't completely keep the rain out, and its feeble row of windows did little toward freshening the gases from their chemical vats in the yard, that would enter the shed itself and build up in a yellow block over their benches. The German chemist Wilhelm Ostwald: "It was a cross between a stable and a potato cellar." It was her province—Pierre's was assimilating this labor—and here, ill-funded and virtually ignored by her scientific peers, she worked her huge piles of dark earth into something that glowed (in December of 1898 Pierre would name it: *radium*). "This miserable shed," she once allowed it to break through her reticence. Her days there could be over twelve hours long, and one winter the temperature sank to and stayed at six degrees above freezing.

But she'd been used to this from her days, not that far past, at the Sorbonne. Her student garret was six flights up, and she climbed them daily like a lab rat in an experiment, for science. In winter she carried the coals up for science, and when the ration of them gave out, she piled her coats on her blankets and shivered blue for science. The water in the washbasin froze overnight and she'd thaw it over her lamp-sized alcohol stove to boil the morning's egg.

And so she was prepared for this. The tons of pitchblende residues arrived from Bohemian mines, dumped into hillocks in the yard like a countryside landscape imported by some eccentric into the heart of Paris. From thousands of gallons of pitchblende liquor she'd distill—and this was her triumph—one lovely thimbleful, literally a thimbleful, of radium. Each batch was "ground, dissolved, filtered, precipitated, collected, redissolved, crystallized, recrystallized . . ." Then more than once in that grimed-up clutter, the small row of porcelain crystallizing bowls would be knocked over, and the whole procedure started anew. You could look around the latch and see her over the fuming cauldrons, transferring products from one to another with an iron bar about as large as she was. "I would be broken with fatigue at the day's end," she once wrote.

And she wrote these were the "best and happiest years of our life." For science. When the heavy sacks from the Joachimstal factory first arrived, she rushed outside and slit the top one open in her eagerness with a little callous-grooming knife from the shop, and thrust her hands in like a child starting a castle at the beach, then running her fingers through the rich brown dust and pine needles, combing it, holding it up to her cheek. "The untroubled quietness of this atmosphere of research and the excitement of actual progress . . . I shall never be able to express the joy."

For this work, this demanding search for a final light, she dressed as she always had in black, or in the near-black "plain dark dress" that she was married in, and which could be worn to the laboratory "and not show dirt." She honeymooned in a black and practical pants-skirt that allowed her bicycling ease, and the black straw hat of those early years remained her single concession to headwear. Almost any diarist's memory of their first being introduced is "somber" . . . "quiet" . . . "composure" . . . "black." The three small linen-covered notebooks of 1897 were black (near a century later, these are still considered *dangerous to handle,* from the first contamination they received at her irradiated fingers). She called the family cat and it slunk to its post at the table leg: a stark little thing of uncompromising black and white.

Because of such garb and a lab routine so strict as to be ritual, it's easy to see her, schematized across the intervening years of popular legend and genre scene, as radium's nun. The Sister of Pure Experiment. Though descriptions normally satisfy themselves with "plain"—you hear it about her, written in this city of fashionability, over and over—but never "severe." So, there was something. I think she hummed, applying a flame to a beaker's residue. She may have hummed a black song, something all the way back to the soil of Poland and down to the black of the bedrock, but I do think she hummed, at least sometimes, in the chill air, serving science.

A thimbleful.

At dinner one night, with a few guests making chitchat in the growing dark, Pierre reached into his waistcoat pocket and brought forth a tube of radium salt.

He held it by the glass lip. The air in the room was the deepening indigo-black of dusk, and the tube gave out its cool blue glow through that with eerie assurance. It highlighted random patches of cuff, of silver tongs, of veal, like a foxfire. Nobody's eyes could leave it. The maid was frozen mid-pour. He turned to her.

"This is the light . . . of the future!"

"Oh Pierre," Marie Curie said drolly.

There are photographs, the two of them in their black clothes posing formally in that turn-of-the-century angular stance, or simply being captured side by side in concentration over a problem of electrical coiling, of adamant formulae not feeding into an answer . . . and their black clothes blend. They make a single body. There is no shadow, no fold, of division. She has many black buttons, a long row down her bosom, that aren't your business or mine.

On some nights they would return to the workshed, standing in the center of its cold, hard, bituminous floor, and be a single dark shape in the dark of the world, and hold their hands, and breaths. The containers were glowing. The bottles of liquid and capsules of crystals shone: faint luminous silhouettes. This she called "enchantment," though she was a woman of empirical method and measurement. Enchantment. All the world was cast in blackness, and here atomic hearts in their bowls shone out.

The everyday life went on. She shopped for a bicycle tire, she oversaw the roast, she signed for an order of sulfur.

She recorded. 5f.50c. for a pair of woolen cycling stockings. 4f.50c. for laundry. 50c. for omnibus travel.

She bathed the baby ("Irène is showing her seventh tooth down on the left"), she paid the nursemaid, she brought back an over-ripe cheese.

The price of three cups of coffee. A booklet of postage stamps. Some lids for the jam.

She purchased a roll of strainer-cloth. She filed the beakers away by size. She mended. She minded.

She answered her mail.

2.

Loie Fuller was writing a letter.

Loie Fuller, the dancer, "living poetry," "hands like the tips of birds' wings," "an enchantress." Her typical evening's bill: "the dance of pearls, in which she entwines herself in strings of pearls taken from the coffin of Heroditas; the snake dance, which she performs in the midst of a wild incantation; the dance of steel, the dance of silver, and dance of fright, which causes her to flee, panic-stricken, from the sight of John's decapitated head persistently following her with martyred eyes."

She began professional dance in burlesque, and in Buffalo Bill's Wild West Show. But her autobiography just refers to this as a period spent "out West." Now she danced at the Folies-Bergere, and for countesses' parties. She danced in skirts 100 silken yards in circumference, manipulated by sticks. She commanded a brisk, select platoon of electricians. Bankers wired her from overseas. Her name appeared on ladies' silk kerchiefs — surely one of the century's earliest star-referent marketing ploys. She danced forty-five minutes straight — fatigued so afterward that the management supplied assistants to carry her home. This was the routine for years.

The Dance of the Meteor.
The Dance of the Flame.
The Dance of the Lily.
The Dance of the Butterfly Wings.

Her *Fifteen Years of a Dancer's Life* is filled with the breathy exclamation of long-protracted girlhood (people and objects are often "exquisite," two or three to a page) and with a charmingly histrionic feel for reportage:

"I am astounded when I see the relations that form and color assume. The scientific admixture of chemically composed colors, heretofore unknown, fills me with admiration, and I stand before them like a miner who has discovered a vein of gold, and who completely forgets himself as he contemplates the wealth of the world before him.

"But to return to my troubles."

And she does.

". . . all that evening I never stopped emitting little groans like those of a wounded animal . . . I was cut to the very quick."

"I cannot describe my despair. I was incapable of words, of gestures. I was dumb and paralysed."

"I trembled all over. Cold perspiration appeared on my temples. I shut my eyes."

"I hated them wildly, and I fell into convulsive tremblings, which shook me from head to foot."

Often, so adventure-crammed is her calendar, this dramatic reaction seems earned, as in "Cologne, where I had to dance in a circus between an educated donkey and an elephant that played the organ. My humiliation was complete." At other times it's the humdrum that's inexplicably fraught with excitement: at an agent's office "I said in a whisper to my mother: 'I am going to knock on the door.' She turned pale, but I had no choice in the matter. My head was in a whirl." She actually did knock, too. "Even if I ran the risk of heart failure."

Ah, but all Loie suffers, she suffers for her Art. She's still very young when she studies herself in the first translucent silk gown, the sun highlighting her body. "This was a moment of intense emotion. Unconsciously I realized that I was in the presence of a great discovery, one which was destined to open the path which I have since followed. Gently, almost religiously, I set the silk in motion, and I saw that I had obtained undulations of a character heretofore unknown." What were they like? Ordinary folk will never know. "You have to see it and feel it. It is too complicated for realization in words."

"I wanted to go to a city where, as I had been told, educated people would like my dancing and would accord it a place in the realm of art." Educated people did. With an awesome intensity, educated people did.

"When I came on the stage each spectator threw a bunch of violets at me. It took five minutes to gather up the flowers. When I was ready to leave the theatre, the students took my horses out of the shafts and drew my carriage themselves, shouting 'Vive l'art! Vive La Loie!'"

"Some days later I was engaged for a performance that was to take place at the hotel in honor of a Russian grand duke, two kings and an empress."

"Just at this time there was presented to me a viscount, who laid claim to my heart and hand."

"On returning to the Hotel Sands, the most beautiful hotel in the city, I found there the municipal orchestra come to serenade me."

Or a party at which "Caruso sang. The courtyard of the hotel had been transformed into a lake, and the host and his guests dined in gondolas."

Most tender and comic both, I think, is the secret, ardent admirer who declares himself by revealing his all: his butterfly collection. "There were 18,000 of them. He pointed out four in particular, and told us he had bought the whole lot for the sake of those, because they looked like me."

In another room are "sixty-two Turners. . . . Finally he came near to me and then, embracing the hall with one big sweep of the hand, said: 'These are your colors. Turner certainly foresaw you when he created them.'"

Art, you see. Art.

Loie first arrived in Paris in 1892. Marie Sklodowska, 1891; she'd struggled her country girl's luggage onto a platform at the

Gare du Nord and the steam from the train, as thick as bunting, was still in her hair a day later as she walked the hill above the Sorbonne. She was like a bag packed full of Poland. She couldn't follow spoken French. But here were the laboratory benches and library shelves of her waking dreams. "A new world opened to me, the world of science." She made no friends. "If sometimes I felt lonely, my usual state of mind was one of calm and great moral satisfaction." That year, it was calculus and physics; the next, elasticity and mechanics. The notes are exact and must have been exacting. In 1893, when she finished her kinematics and electrostatics studies and went on to her final examination, to take first place as *licenciée èn physiques,* Loie Fuller was also transplanting her chosen learning to Gallic soil. The sun through Notre Dame's famous windows "enchanted me more than anything else . . . I quite forgot where I was. I took my handkerchief from my pocket, a white handkerchief, and I waved it in the beams of colored light, just as in the evening I waved my silken materials in the rays of my reflectors." This fervent rapture, however, displeases a watchful cathedral attendant, who leads the young danseuse back out: "To be brief he dropped me on to the pavement." The world is rich in schools and lessons.

Of Loie's learning, of Loie's theory of historical verisimilitude . . . She's asked about her claim to recreate the ancient dances of the Hindus and Egyptians. "There are very few documents treating of the subject, but it seems to me that it should be easy," she answers in a snap, "if one put oneself in the state of mind that prompted the dances in times past, to reproduce them today with similar action and movement. If the custom still existed of dancing at funerals, a little reflection will show that the dances would have to suggest and express sadness, despair, grief, agony, resignation and hope." I see a board of French archaeologists shudder at these assumptions — it passes down the line of them one at a time, like the shimmy of second-string Folies chorines in a sensual-comic glissando . . . Or would they applaud and shower their novice scholar with nosegays? Likability was an aura about her. Admit it: you're coming to like her. The most extraordinary assemblage liked her.

There was, it seems, this empathy. At sixteen she inveigles her way to a closed performance of Sarah Bernhardt's. From somewhere in the audience: "I believe I understood her soul, her life, her greatness. She shared her personality with me." Later, though still a stranger to the language, she meets Alexandre Dumas. "Instead of taking one of his hands I grasped both emphatically. From this time on a great friendship, a great sympathy, subsisted between us, although we were unable to understand each other."

One night (by now she's conversant in French) the astronomer Flammarion, cartographer of Mars and founding father of *L'Astronomie,* is among the crowd in her dressing-room. Dumas is also present:

" 'Is it possible that the two most distinguished personalities in Paris are not acquainted with each other?'

" 'It is not so remarkable,' replied Dumas, 'for, you see, Flammarion dwells in space, and I am just a cucumber of the earth.'

" 'Yes,' said Flammarion, 'but a little star come out of the West has brought us together.' "

Rodin tours Loie through his "temple of art." The Princess of Roumania feels a sympathetic bond before her guest has spoken three sentences: "Do you think that a princess should always be cold and ceremonious when she receives a stranger? Well, so far as I am concerned, you are not a stranger at all. After having seen you in your beautiful dances it seems to me that I am well acquainted, and I am very glad indeed that you have come to see me."

She came to see them, or they came to see her. The one would almost inevitably ensure the other. This was Paris, 1904, and bountiful with human stars in a way Flammarion's nighttime skies could never really match. They dazzled. Want it or not, the lines of constellations would be established between them. Rumor. Handbills. The more sensational press. Loie Fuller was writing a letter.

Everybody was talking about it, "radium" this and "radium" that. Perhaps it could be used to light a costume from a blackened stage? She would need enough for—oh, ten yards to start . . . The table's candle flame was prismed to a dozen dancing harem girls, crystal and gold in her inkwell. They would be flattered. She would be flattered. They would picnic together and talk in one exuberant voice about Art. Monsieur and Madame Curie, she began . . .

"Refused, she experimented with a phosphorescent pigment which blew part of her hair off and caused her landlord to evict her."

But exchange of letters continued. Should you care to meet . . . Yes, very much so . . . They met. There was this empathy.

3.

I go to bed thinking two expatriate women walking a Paris street . . . there's an organ-grinder, just like in that grainy, ebullient photograph by Atget . . . and the door to an absinthe bar, with luscious female seraphs framing the fanlight . . . A drizzle has left the air sweet. One woman uses her hands, as if molding her very American French in front of her, tucking it here, adorning it there . . . The other's hands are clasped behind her — the way her hair is in a bun has become a model for her body — and every now and then there's just an understanding *oui,* and a brief smile like a secret dossier eked open for a peek . . .

Then I drift into sleep with them, true to my wife already asleep beside me, but sleeping with them too, nonetheless. They're speaking Spanish now. They're walking the streets of Paris, *rues* A through Z, and speaking Spanish. One's a man. It's crazy. Sleep does that. Now I'm on the deck of a ship. We're watching the dolphins. One of us is the man, and one the lady, but which is which? "They make a dotted line of the sea," she says or he says or I say — in Spanish, although the high school Spanish I really know is relegated strictly to saying I had fried eggs for breakfast. "That must be the contract God signs every day." It's a good rejoinder. And then we go visit a castle together, the organ-grinder's whiny tootle fading in and out and in again . . .

Sleep does that. I remember when I was in seventh grade Joel Rosenblatt showed me his father's ham radio. All of those voices, all of those strangers, all night long in so many languages, thousands of miles apart yet overlapping on the frequency band . . . all that, and one man plugged into reception.

> *Conchita Jurado was a penniless, gray-haired, bespectacled schoolteacher, who during her sixty-seven years led a fabulous double-life that kept Mexico's high society spinning. Masquerading as the elegant Don Carlos Balmori, the wealthiest living Spaniard, famed duelist, big-game hunter, owner of railways and castles in Spain, Conchita began her career by disguising herself as a young suitor and appearing before her own father to ask for her hand. As Don Carlos, she was the center of a mysterious and exclusive society known as Las Balmori, whose members were those who had been duped by Don Carlos. The club membership fostered the Don Carlos reputation by passing out $100 and $1000 checks. Each year now the memory of Don Carlos is revived (in December) with a pilgrimage to Conchita's grave.*
>
> — *Terry's Guide to Mexico,* 1926

Halfway through the night I wake. My wife is speaking gibberish. Again, in her sleep, the neurons discharging through language, as they must do for the zealously mystic who "speak in tongues." I've seen films of them, flopping like fish on the floor, the gods taking over their speech.

And I've read studies — how, panculturally, the gibberish has a pattern, of chemical storage and release. If you plug into that deepest frequency, if primal jack and primal outlet meet in the world of molecular structures and fit, perhaps the language opens up into something shimmering and accessible. Perhaps two women, who shouldn't by any of this world's rules have any ground in common, walk a Paris street in intimate conversation we'd find impossible, opaque.

On a level of chemicals or gods, my wife is surely saying something of vast importance — her voice is plaintive, her forehead is trying to make a fist. I think in that world her sister is dying again — thirty-four years old, my age. I think she dies again every night, and will for a while. I think if I knew the secrets of infant grammar shared worldwide despite the parents' language, if I could crack the code of schizophrenic babble in locked wards going back to the first dark raving we made in the caves . . . But I don't know Spanish, even.

And how many nights did Conchita Jurado wake mid-syllable, not sure, in the surrounding confusion of insectwhirr and starclutter, which of her selves she was, and who'd begun that sentence?

Now I realize why the Spanish *r* and *tilde* colored the chatter of my Francophilic dreamstreets—I'd been going over that snippet in *Terry's Guide,* a note for a possible poem to follow my Curie prose piece, and it stuck in the gym-sole bottom of my brain. Sleep does that. It's crazy. I think if . . .

"The clock in the radio." Now it's come to words I know, and soon (this much of the pattern I understand) she'll quiet speechlessly back to true sleep. For these few moments, though, it's the clock in the radio, over and over, whatever that is, wherever, and she wants it desperately much. The clock. In the radio.

Something to do about Time. About the reception of Voices.

On any day at Niagara Falls, the crowd shows a wild variety. I was there on one of those rare unexpected springlike days in December, and the wall of spray at the Rainbow Falls admitted a perfect arc of the spectrum, each of its colors in strident declaration. The couples kept coming: in turbans, in leather jackets, in tuxes and low-cut gauze concoctions, one pair was a business suit and a kimono . . .

But on the Canadian side you can tour the tunnels cut into the very rock, and for this you need to buy a ticket, take the elevator down and, in a long and smelly locker room especially designed for nothing but metamorphosis, suit up in clumsy rubber.

They're solid yellow or solid black, and all alike from hood to boots. Remember grammar school street crossing guards, out in the rain? The suit is enormous—it's like a small room about you, a room in the shape of a fireplug. The cuff of its sleeve is guaranteed to hit exactly the middle of your palm, and you're a child again, in second grade, in a shirt too large, as if everything wasn't anyway in those days made to diminish you . . .

Your fingers show, and a strip of eyes—it's all that's left of your earlier self. Then you walk out into the world of your duplicates . . . This was more amazing a sight for me than the water, though that's amazing enough, the endless tons of lace, the pummel of lace that could kill you.

The tunnels are dim and always vibrating in the roar of rock being violently worn. The air there is water, the water there is the air, it's that simple. By this time you're one of a hundred comic book sperm up their designate tubule—each alike and each carrying, deep inside, an individuation.

You look. Now anyone could be someone else.

I think that's true, or partly true, for all of us, and what we call "friendship" or saying "we felt like sisters" or "it's as if I could read his mind" is the everyday version of more extreme occasion. But first it requires this facelessness stage, these tunnels, a swim inside the primary origin-goop.

I think Conchita Jurado would know this. I think she's been there, often, and back. I think there's an atom of this Niagara Falls between a man and a woman in any real marriage, beyond the honeymoon suite and the tacky photo of both of you loonily waving from inside a fake barrel going over fake water's long plunge . . . one white, commingling osmosis-atom of this Niagara Falls.

She wakes in the Mexican morning and knows intuitively who she'll be today—some regal Blue, or a passionate Red deep-shading into Scarlet, or a domestic Yellow . . . She knows, and dances with great elation into a room where grapefruit halves are scrubbing the air with their scent. She's spent the night, again, in a place where colors blend back to the first White Light, and now she knows enough to start to know how it breaks, into faces.

Though she's not anyone yet, for me—I place her note in a pile, under the clipping in which the poet H.D. is on deck watching dolphins, I have more immediate needs. I've been writing a while already—writing Fuller, writing her letters—and when I pass the bedroom door on the way to my study, I see that Morgan's awake. The hair close in at her temples is damp from a tough night.

"You were talking again. 'The radio in the clock.'"

"Oh Albear," she says, just that, and rubs it all out of her eyes, and is fully returned.

That's her name for me: Albear.

Her sister's dead of cystic fibrosis at thirty-four, my age, my calendrical might-have-been, my other. Death makes a kind of sensitivity in the living, and you think that way for a while. For Morgan it's more extreme, the love having been extreme. She has her own, genetic, might-have-been she has to learn to live with.

The others are everywhere. How many angels can dance in the head of a man? The others are everywhere, the way we're always walking through thousands of radio voices though rarely picking much up. It doesn't require death. It might be just a husband kissing a wife and there isn't a clear-cut border. Simply, two women might walk down a Paris street. It's a springlike day in December. They're happy, though only one is obviously carefree; the other is like a tune in a music box painted pure black and her friend is figuring how the crank works. She points, with a whoop, to where it streaks cleanly out of a cloud.

"In English we call this *Rain. Bow.*"

4.

"In Polish, *teçza.*"

She started naming things in Polish as they caught her eye, the cart of mannequins wheeling toward a boutique, the flavored ices in the vendor's wagon by color, an organ-grinder in his crumpled amoeba-shaped cap, she gave each name and then a pause that pushed up against the name like a mark of punctuation, so it was as if she were reading out figures on a chart. But Loie started to give the English as a counterpoint, and made it into a singsong, and in a moment they were skipping down the twisting byway hand in hand, singing bilingual duets, a book stall, a bicycle, a string of beads, a puddle, a splash, an oops, for this we say "oops."

They sat on a park bench letting their hems dry. Loie knew some of Poland's famed, exiled women. She'd met the actress Modjeska, the Countess Wolska . . . It was in her student days, they seemed so lost to her now, that Marie Curie cut herself off from even the meaningful walks with other Warsaw students, rambling the Latin Quarter with Poland's gilded saints and feisty sausages filling their talk . . . It returned to her now, and for a little while she couldn't do more but sit with its sweet weight pressing down. They watched a corner hustler switch his pea confusingly under three silver cups, and a group of tourists guessing. But the two of them were quiet, Loie seeming to understand this rush of reverie.

When they walked on, there were other topics: light, how light exulted a woman working it through her silks; how there would sometimes be a phial of light in the shed at night like a single finger caught pointing the way to an Answer of Answers . . . Loie felt lifted a mile, to be taken as an equal by someone like this, to talk of—she'd write it this way in her diary—"deep things." Marie Curie felt opened an inch. She'd even let her visitor pin a flower to her blouse. For what they meant, they were equal—that mile, that inch—and the two walked back to the Curies'.

Loie wouldn't be welcomed into the laboratory; it wasn't a mixing like that. But she was served a decent wine in the parlor at 108 Boulevard Kellermann, Pierre uncorking the neck with all of the naive flair of a child magician's first try at the rabbit and the hat. Then there were little soulful cheeses and one plate apiece of sardines.

Loie told her adventures until the sun set: When she was stranded, without a penny or crust of bread, at the Russian border ("I walked up and down in the darkness like a caged beast"). When, on a lark, she locked a testy French reporter in her stateroom, effectively kidnapping him to America ("At first he protested, not without vehemence, but he soon cooled off and gaily assumed his part in the rather strenuous farce into which we had precipitated him"). When she arranged the escape of the lovely actress Hanako, from a low-life Antwerp dive ("where she had to sing and dance for the amusement of sailors"). When "a magnificent negro, six feet high, who looked like some prince from the Thousand and One Nights" showed her the Senegalese sunset prayer—and, as the sun *was* setting then, the Curies' parlor saw a demonstration of those sinuous prostrations. Such things! Who could imagine?

For their turn, after much prodding, Pierre read a paper. "This is special, Loie, for us. Pierre inscribed a copy of this very study and made it a present to me, the first present, after we met. Pierre?" He stood and cleared his throat. "On symmetry in physical phenomena: symmetry in an electric field and in a magnetic field," he began. Loie was in heaven.

It was late enough then, time to send Irène to sleep and for Loie to meet her carriage.

"Irène, dis bonne nuit à Mademoiselle Loie."

"Bonne nuit, Mamselle."

"Bonne nuit."

That April, having returned from a tour of Vienna, she took them to visit Rodin.

The short, bull-muscled man extended his hand and Loie introduced the three to one another, the names, and then a trading of everyday *bonjour,* and then a hush, as if the gate to a tunnel of silence. The sculptor motioned, a cock of his overlarge and overbearded head, and they followed up the hill to his studios, the "temple."

These were the rooms in which Rodin had naked models wander freely, to catch each tense, each blued-over bruise's rise and relax, each nipple's stiffen or sleep, in absolute candor. He'd said, "People say I think too much about women. Yet after all, what is there more important to think about?" He'd said, "No good sculptor can model a human figure without dwelling on the mystery of life." He'd said, "The mouth, the luxurious protruding lips sensuously eloquent — here the perfumed breath comes and goes like bees darting in and out of a hive." One of his Balzacs held a kingly hard-on in its hand.

And here he was, silently pointing to this small bronze of a dancer, to that wax study of Eve, to the life-size couple in such an erotic clasp, the veins in the marble surely held blood . . . and running his hands across the stone, the dimples in stone, the swelling hips of stone, until they were flesh, until he wasn't polishing but kneading . . .

Was she shocked, this quiet daughter of Warsaw? *Yes.* Was she quickened, was something in her raised and made raw by these figures pushing at life as if *it* were the stone? *Yes*. Did she walk the halls with Loie hand in hand, like sisters? *Yes*. But Loie still, and only, called her "Madame Curie," isn't that so? *Yes*. Were they two studies of one woman? *Yes, in different media, by different artists, under different stars*.

"In the two hours we passed in the temple hardly ten words were spoken."

"Missyoor, M'dahm Cur*eeey*."

They both ran from the kitchen to the parlor. She was on the sofa, sitting in the posture of *The Thinker,* eyes enormously crossed.

That night she insisted on dancing for them, a private show for two, "since your labors will not permit the theater." She would do three numbers "providing Madame will assist me in wardrobe preparations between the acts, yes?" (1) A medley of her most famous creations. (2) *The Harlequinade,* a comic number still in preparation ("If smiles bud *here,* my friends, at the Folies they will blossom."). (3) *The Dance of Science-Light,* in special tribute to her hosts. "There will be no orchestra, nor my intricate light arrangements. But you will allow me to place the lamps like so . . .? Our spirits will know the music."

His wife returned in a few minutes, sitting next to him. (The warm quip from their friends at the School of Physics: that they sat like the halves of a balanced equation.) A minute more, and Loie appeared.

The space of the lucent parabolas she defined was disproportionate to the space of the parlor; every kick and swivel she performed had been invented for different dimensions. Even so, an eerie beauty entered the room with her; and in her floating sashes and sleeves, as they circled the sofa as if with wings or whipped at her ankles like egg whisks, air and oil light were wed phantasmagorically. At times the light in the colored silks took on the solid shapeliness of Rodin's hand-sized bronze dancers, like attendant putti about her in a cloud.

She was a meteor, then a flame, then a lily, then butterfly wings . . . A dream came back to Marie Curie, not whole cloth, but a tatter of dream. Something . . . "A premonition of tonight," she thought. And then rethought it, in more appropriate metaphor, "A rehearsal of tonight's performance." Pierre let go her hand and she went to help with the alien underpinnings.

"The Harlequinade. The clown imagines herself a regent, and struts to her own discomforture." Yes, they did smile. She was a tatterdemalion pixie-toes in pratfalls now, was bundles of motley thrown in arabesques. The first performance had left them unsure of proper response, but when Pierre let go her hand this time they both clapped like children at carnival doings. He heard his wife laugh all the way out of the parlor and into the changing room, it might have been Irène with a playmate.

Again, Pierre was alone. The final number now, *The Dance*— what was it? —*of Science-Light*. A high kick out of the doorway, and the hands upraised to make a single timeless, faceless incense-smoke of the body, a gray gauze crazily spinning and seeming to rise—faster, fervent, almost clumsy in fervency, very clumsy and very fervent, throwing energy off in radiant chunks, the face a faintish glow in mist and then the arms dropping heavily down and she curtsied in front of him, still by himself, and breathless from her effort. "Marie."

5.

But by then Pierre couldn't applaud without pain. As early as 1898 the aches had started, the lethargy and the reddened, tender fingertips. He was put on a special diet for "his rheumatism." She had gone in for a lung examination and sputum analyses.

Lifting a test tube was painful. Dressing himself was very painful, at times. Nobody knew. They were the first. On June 19, 1903, Pierre had addressed the Royal Institution in London, summarizing their radium experiments, and adding to this with tricks from a tube: its light, its altering a wrapped photographic plate. A week later, he wrote to thank the institution—his fingers could hardly grip the pen. Fifty years later, the presence of the radium could still be detected in parts of the institution, which needed decontamination.

Her weaknesses came and went and reappeared. His legs trembled. A colleague in radium, Friedreich Giesel, discovered his breath alone touched off an electroscope. The violet marks of burn continued appearing. A touch could do it. These were occupational hazards, little purplish medals won in the quest toward explicating the atom. Pierre had a permanent scar, he spent long bouts of spasm in bed. It was his rheumatism; it happened "because of the damp in our shed."

They were the first. And so nobody knew: about the clocks of cancer it set ticking in the marrow, about the shredding of the fibers of the lungs. Expectant mothers today, if they work in the radium industry, are cautioned not to expose their bodies to greater than .03 rem per week. But she must have been absorbing one full rem per week, a lady in a black dress pouring from flask to flask. The gamma radiation tests were in the future, the radon tests were in the future, far in the future, and nobody knew. On December 11, 1903: "My husband has been to London to receive the Davy Medal which has been given to us. I did not go with him for fear of fatigue." They were going to have their second child. From flask to flask. In August that year, on a bicycling trip, in a cheap room in a seaside hotel, she broke into early labor. It was dead—a girl—in an hour. "There is no direct evidence for the cause."

In November that year, they won the Nobel Prize. The 70,000 francs would support new radium research. The rector of the Academy of Paris was in touch: Pierre was to have his own lab, with a small support staff, and his wife "would receive a salary for the first time in her career." But for the banquets and the autograph hounds and the agents who wrote of lecture tours and the melodramatic headlines in the press, they had no time. They were weak, they were busy; they needed to seek, in strictest purity, the submost script on the blueprints of creation. Marchand, the French Minister in Stockholm, received the prize on their behalf. "One would like to dig into the ground somewhere to find a little peace."

They dug in, they worked. She became pregnant again and bore Eve, who was healthy. "The children are growing well," she writes her brother in 1905, and goes on: how they'd cry, and how she'd rock them quiet. Robert Reid, her biographer, adds: "But they were not the center-point of her life." For feminist causes she had no patience. They both refused to reap a penny of personal gain from their labor. There were bits below the bits below the pulses circling in an atom, and they dug in, and they worked, at what she called, in the early days, "our legitimate scientific dream."

They dreamed, they dug in, they worked. He studied effects of radioactive emanations on mice and guinea pigs—the pulmonary congestions, the weakening leukocytes. That his body was also a guinea pig's for science, his papers never hinted. Nobody knew. What might have happened, given time, to this upright man with his life on fire, nobody will ever know. There wasn't time. On April 19, 1906, while crossing Rue Dauphine in an afternoon rain, he slipped in the path of a horse cart. The driver, a Louis Manin, was weeping as the gendarmerie arrived. His left rear wheel had smashed Pierre Curie's head into fifteen or sixteen pieces.

"The fragile brain," he once called it. Now it was on view in a run of gutter water and blood. She took the news and later identified the body with that reserve the world had come to expect. There were no tears for the journalists from her, nor did her own hurt hands torment themselves in public.

But alone in the upstairs room, she started a diary, really the first love letters she'd ever attempted. She wrote to the dead man. "What a terrible shock your poor head has felt, that I have so often caressed in my two hands. I kissed your eyelids which you used to close so that I could kiss them . . ." She led her sister Bronia into the bedroom. There was a packet wrapped in waterproof paper and in it, the bloodstained clothes. Dried flesh was stuck to the garments. She started kissing these little discolored remains of her husband, tenderly, repeatedly, until Bronia grabbed them and threw them into the fire . . . And now, she allowed herself tears.

"Within two weeks of the death she was dealing with correspondence concerning the future of her laboratory, and within a month her laboratory notebook starts again . . . precipitating, purifying, observing emanations, and always measuring—hour after hour."

This is the work for which she was awarded a second Nobel Prize—the first person ever so double-awarded. The simple initial picture of the atom's innards was being filled in. The International Radium Standard was being methodically formulated. Radium and polonium were established in the periodic table of elements. These were the years of her giving definitive shape to the start of the nuclear age, and the eyes of these years would see her as the autocratic, unyielding prima donna in black—"not a very nice person," as a British physicist put it.

Her own eyes would fail—cataracts, four precarious operations and at their end a thick pair of pebble glasses. The ureter infection. The open sores. A worker in her labs in the old days, Demenitroux, dead at forty-four of pernicious anemia. Theodore Blum, a New York dentist, recognized the cancerous jaws of woman after woman: years of licking the tips of brushes dipped in radium paint, for watches with luminous hands. He named it "radium jaw." The bad news wouldn't stop, or her fears, or her conscience.

Irène was a woman now, her own doctoral thesis presented successfully at the Sorbonne. These were, in a way, the years of fulfillment. At the 1911 Solvay Conference, two solemn rows of civilization's most eminent living physicists are posed for the camera—twenty-nine men and a woman. She and Einstein stand (four faces away from each other) in the back. Jacob Bronowski: "Here the great age opens. Physics becomes in those years the greatest collective work of art of the twentieth century." And here, at the fifth of the Conferences, in 1927, one year before the death of Loie Fuller, she and Einstein have moved to the first, the seated, row. There are twenty-eight men and a woman. The International Radium Standard Unit was, and is, the *curie*.

"35f.25c. for the black (lace) dress in which to go to meet the President of the United States . . ."

But there are moments when something else is required, something other.

Loie had written: breast cancer. All of the surgeons wanted to cut it off, but one, who said that radium needles would surely cure it. What, please, what did Madame recommend?

—Nothing helpful, nothing lucid, only the name of her own physician, Regaud, and her love, and her wishes. The thank you was "tremblingly scrawled" to her: "Dear, dear friend. Once again in your debt."

She remembered . . . walking, the halls at Rodin's, Pierre on one side of her, Loie the other. Wasn't there something . . . *a pea,* beneath three silver cups, a seed, from one to the other . . .

It was a warm night under a peach moon even her filmed-over eyes couldn't dim. It was an empathetic night. She felt so hopeless, and out in the garden she made her hands into a basket shape, for carrying such a burden. She bowed her shoulders low, and then bent to the ground with her lips in the cared-for grasses and sobbed and said his name to him in a soundless calling that tasted of dirt and early April green, and then she was up again, and facing the moon and whatever impossible powers peopled its darker side, and here was a fist for the moon, and here were two arms open to anything shining, anything bright that the sky had to offer her, even if it burned, the light could take her now, she dared it to, the light that was only a milk in her eyes but a coal in her gut could lift her if it wanted to, she was ready now . . .

Irène looked out of the mullioned glass. It was something she had never seen before (although it had happened, once, before). Her mother was dancing.

. . . it seems to me that it should be easy, if one put oneself in the state of mind that prompted the dances in the past, to reproduce them today with similar action and movement. If the custom still existed of dancing at funerals, a little reflection will show that the dances would have to suggest and express sadness, despair, grief, agony, resignation and hope.

6.

Peter Van Eck was a more mysterious affair. She first met him in 1920 *on the trip to Greece. At one point she called it "a conventional meeting or voyage-out romance," but she never seemed very sure whether he really appeared, or she dreamt him altogether or partially, or if he was a supernatural visitation. Moreover, he appeared to have had a double, whom she called "the Man on the boat," who resembled Van Eck, but not closely enough for certainty. The most interesting encounter occurs when, after a nap in the afternoon, she goes out on deck, where she meets Van Eck. Her uncertainty about him is described as ambiguously as possible, even to the quality of light: "He is older — no, he must be younger. But it is near-evening, it is this strange light. But the light is not strange," and so on. Then they watch some dolphins together, swimming in "a curiously unconvincing pattern."*

— KENNETH FIELDS,
on the poet H.D.

"They make a dotted line of the sea," H.D. says.

"That must be the contract God signs every day," Van Eck says, if he's there, or if he isn't there, or his double says or doesn't say. Anyway, it's a good rejoinder.

They both lean on the rail a while, fading in and out of the evening light — as if being stitched through the light. Perhaps on the light's other side, the effect is the same: they're there, then gone, and here for a moment.

"Do you understand?" says Van Eck.

"Quién sabe?" she says back, in the voice of Conchita Jurado. Although I only know Spanish enough to ask for two fried . . .

"Eggs?" It's the stewardess, waking me up.

Breakfast.

I'm in a plane

going home, from Vermont, where I've been for four strange days to give a reading of my work. I think I read well, the response was sweet, and afterwards we ate Chinese in delicious, imperial portions. The weather was lovely enough to keep me delaying departure — the way the sky is a blue cream floating on top of those hills. But I knew it was time to go because I woke with my wife's face softly pressed against mine although I was alone in the bed, had been alone four nights a thousand miles away from her. You know what I mean. We all know, in ways and at times. I felt that gentle sleeping breathing of hers, and felt the wrinkle she gives behind it every few minutes. And so I knew, and I picked up my check and packed.

I do believe in a sloppily mystical way that people can share a face; or a face can travel beyond its body; or there is a single Face, of which *our* faces are pieces. Such stuff aside, there are Siamese twins. There are binary stars. Personae. There is a dancer in a role, and it doesn't end at her pores; we wouldn't want it any other way.

I think if all of these faces at 7:00 A.M. around me slurping coffee could be overlapped, we'd make white light—but first we'd need that closeness. There's a stepping-up of value through diminishment, as in: the amount of gold or gourmet truffle on the market; anything "cute"; or a plane as the distance around it increases. We taxi and lift, another clumsy tube of human cargo circling out of the Burlington Airport, and start to shrink by the 20,000 foot level, so compacted by endless space around us we must become the heaviest thing in the universe—only the eye of a deity could hold such weight, and even the eye of a deity couldn't keep our faces from blending. Smaller, and more transparent, and smaller—a single, sunny floater in the peripheral vision of God.

But there's another way to say it:

It was a warm night under a peach moon. It was an empathetic night. Loie signaled (a foot tap) and the first notes of *The Harlequinade* rose perkily from her flautist, then the piano came in. The crowd was large and very receptive, and after two dramatic acts they normally loved this wackier number. "The clown imagines herself a regent . . ." She took a breath, leapt onstage

and felt all of the weight of age and lack of option on her shoulders. Now she knew she should be twirling—she saw the conductor, he started the twirling bit—but here she was, shaping her hands in a basket, for carrying such a burden. She bowed her shoulders low, and then bent to the stage with her lips in imagined grasses and sobbed and called a far-off name — the orchestra was puzzled now, but trying to pace her, slowing itself and deepening — and then she was up, and facing the moon and whatever impossible powers peopled its darker side, and here was a fist for the moon, the audience stunned by the energy, some of the women openly weeping and then a few of the men, and here were two arms open to anything shining, anything bright that the sky had to offer, her orchestra silent completely now and the audience starting to give voice to its feeling in a communal moaning, even if it burned, the light could take her now, she dared it to, then cheering although the dance wasn't done yet, on its feet like a single huge animal cheering, the light could lift her if it wanted to, yes, she was ready now . . .

and falling spent to her greatest applause, where we'll leave her

in notes for a poem I'm doing, 20,000 feet up. I file her brusquely away in a pile of scraps that keep slipping over my "tray-table" — documentation.

The Indian (also New Guinean and Philippine) fireflies flash in simultaneity — a dense swarm in a tree will go off as if comprising a single brain being charged by a single great thought; the lag from one to another is, at the most, 20 milliseconds. / Or how about fish? Of about 20,000 species, over 10,000 school. I've seen a school of 10 like shiny dimes, that moved as whole as a dollar bill. / There is communication we don't understand yet, bird to bird down a V, though our mouths go *oh!,* our cells go *oh!,* in its presence. In one experiment Russian scientists took a momma rabbit far offshore and deep, in a submarine. Colleagues slit the throats of her babies, one by one. Invariably, she set her electrodes registering like crazy at the proper second. / It can't be surprising a sleeping mother wakes in response to a cry from the crib and finds the first few beads of lactation have started already — Kathy tells me, Mimi, Janis, Joelle. / The novelist John Cowper Powys told Theodore Dreiser, on leaving his home, "I'll appear before you, right here, later this evening. You'll see me." Dreiser did, quite clearly, hours later — and right then phoned up

Powys's house in the country, a leisurely train ride off. Powys answered. It can't be surprising. There is communication. / There is a traveling out of the body reported through time in a legacy library-large. August Strindberg believed the astral body of his third wife, Harriet Bosse, would arrive in his room at night and masturbate him. Other cases are less suspicious than this, or contain an intra-verification; the monk Alphonsus Liguori, in 1774, reported sleeping and sending an astral projection four hours away, to Rome, where he said the pope had just died. The pope *had* just died, it turned out. And those who attended his final minutes "had seen and talked to Liguori, who led the prayers for the Pontiff." / It crosses death. Conan Doyle—whose Holmes is an exemplum of the rational, empirical process, skepticism and model objectivity—received, through his wife Jean, letters from his dead son Kingsley "in childish scrawl." Yeats' wife Georgie did similarly—as if her pencil came from the wood of an ancient threshold between two worlds. Rosemary Brown transcribed new compositions by Liszt, Beethoven, Chopin, Brahms, Schubert, did a program for the BBC and made a record: "Mrs. Brown is not a skilled musician; she does not even have a gramophone in her house" and yet "her" compositions "could be considered practically first quality by the particular composer." One frowns, one shakes one's head and continues to measure the den for linoleum tiles. But toward the end of his life, that consummate man of measurement, Monsieur Pierre Curie, researched spiritualism. X rays, radium, ectoplasmic appearances . . . they were one world then, for him, for others. On tour in Britain, Conan Doyle spoke to 150,000. *Of course* they half-believed. They dreamed. Some took the wafer on Sunday. Every one of them had turned around once, sure he was being watched, and he was, and you have too, admit it. You would have bought a ticket. / It doesn't have to be so mystical, so much the rapping table or the clank in the night. I mean any kid alone in the playground talking to his invisible friends. I *know* they aren't there. You tell *him*. I had a dalmatian named PeeWee who could change his size a dozen fold at will. / The dwarf spy Richebourg, who could pass as a baby, and so smuggled messages out of the tumultuous France of 1789; arrived in a friendly house, he'd whip the dispatch out from his baby-blue quilt, politely burp, and light up a cigar. How many people was he, how many can anyone be? / The study *Sybil* "describes a total of 17 personalities" living in one crowded, fractured mind — there are about 100 cases of so-called "split personality" in psychiatric literature, from Mary Reynolds (1817) to now. / What inspired rapport does it take for an archaeologist, turning some lumpish inscrutable object of unknown use, to suddenly see it with Neolithic eyes and scream *lamp!* or *sickle sharpener!* / Everyone travels. A shaman lives "in his actual tribal world and in the sacred world of Primordial Beings" and writhes with it and says he flies, but everyone travels — you're here with me right now and we've come a long way, haven't we?

20,000 feet up.

There is this empathy.

Though I'd rather just say it this way: I'm a man coming home and I'd rather say just these two simple things:

I've checked out of a hotel, which is a stable state for endless flux of bodies.

And I've had Chinese food. Those fortune cookies: little curled up sleepers holding their common bits of tomorrow. They could be anyone.

Then Morgan's picking me up at the airport. Back home, I file the notes away. I'll start it tomorrow (I don't have a title yet) if an opening scene, some line from Curie, comes. But for now, I need to catch up with the last four days of my own life, which kept running here like a lamp left on, while I had another life, four days complete, in Vermont.

Phone messages, letters from friends . . . I'm hours at writing back to them.

"So. What was Vermont like? Poetry groupies?"

"Morgel . . ."

That's what I call her: The Morgel.

After our holding each other, she drops off to sleep (she's worked a full day, then gone with me through luggage-grief at the American Airlines complaint desk). In a while I see her REMs — like eyes that are reading by braille. She gets letters from people I'll never know, letters she'll never remember.

Then later, from out of her sleep: "Goodnight, Albear."

Bonne nuit. "Now,"

the poet Jon Anderson says,
"In the middle of my life,
A woman of delicate bearing gives me
Her hand, & friends
Are so enclosed within my reasoning
I am occasionally them."

I wake up. It's dark. I can't even see you beside me. I can't see me. I lay in this darkness a while, and feel something thin and nearly weightless, a kind of film, on my face, and shaped to my face's arrangement of muscle perfectly. It must be I grow used to it after a while, or maybe it simply sinks in. Wasn't I going to turn to you and ask for the pen and paper, to take down jottings for my prose poem? It must be through my skin and in my blood by now, though just a few minutes have passed. I feel my lips make their first stretchy part of the night's accretion of sealants, and then it's my voice: "I'll need the condenser plates, syringes and electrometer."

Author's Note: My inspiration was a mention of Loie Fuller in Barbara Barker's article "Sources for the Dance Historian in the Hoblitzelle Theatre Arts Library." From that, I went on to Robert Reid's fascinating biography *Marie Curie,* and Loie Fuller's autobiography *Fifteen Years of a Dancer's Life*. Without those two sources, "Fuller" wouldn't have been half full. The two women did know each other, amicably. Many of the events of their unique rapport are, however, of my own imagination.

Threshold

Every dollop says "dybbuk" or "God." —These thirteenth-to fifteenth-century Hebrew manuscript illustrations. Here's the fourteen-volume legal code, the *Mishneh Torah,* inscribed by Nathan ben Simeon ha-Levi: deep blue tendrils from its topmost words curve delicately down to frame the entire frontispiece page. So jurisprudence, even, is given its dreamlife and soul. The larger letters hold birds, and dainty dragons the size of the birds.

Even on the butchery floor as one man checks the fresh slit in a slaughtered ox to certify it kosher, with the bored finesse of a customs official rummaging luggage; even in the pantry's standard run of ritual candelabra, incense pans and ram's horns; even over by the barley field, ribby goats being whipped across the unsurprising horizon of rabbis and herring vendors, boys at hooky, someone axing cedar . . . Holy writ is superlunary and geological, filling the air, the earth, the margins.

Ruth is gleaning wheat. The Biblical Ruth, the famous one. And there are other threshers, too, in daily labor: with a basket, or a rake, or bundling sheaves as firm as quivers of freshly-fletched arrows. We're too far to see the ordinary sweat across this ordinary toil, though we understand that this is a scene of routine effort applied to routine need. Yes, but Ruth has the head of a cat. One worker bent in shears-sharp silhouette has the head of a hawk. The first word, *va-ye-heé,* in letters the size of garden gates, floats eye-high through the wheat of this picture.

And everywhere, the script of The Lord's Own Say-So is a black flock winging overhead, is neat black coal seams underground. These pictures say the earth we walk on *is* the Pentateuch—if we'll see it that way. The sky with its text-bearing seraphs, showers of manna, spirits wearing blinding uniforms of fire, is the air we breathe—if we'll breathe it that way.

I.

Six or seven well-kept avenues radiated loosely from my block. (I was six or seven, or so, myself. The year, let's say, is 1955.) The neighborhood was lower middle-class, and I suppose its wants were: scrabbling to a next step up the socioclimb; its fears were: slipping off some flung banana skin of misfortune and landing smack on the poorhouse floor. What I remember mainly, though, is not so much a movement higher or lower in status, but just a daily kind of frantic male-workforce and female-housework treadmill-run to stay in place. This meant, in both arenas, a labored show of propriety, saying we were better than what was below us and worthy of what was above. The aqua fake fur slip-on covers for the kleenex boxes matched the fake fur of the toilet tank.

And those avenues—they generally were goal-specific, and generally those goals were foursquare and sunlit. One road took you to the grade school, one to the Buy-N-Bag, they were known not by their street sign names (Ainslie, meaning who-knew-what) but by their approved destinations: "Take the Bank Street, only turn a block before you reach the Bank . . ." The avenue handing me over, block by block, to Sunday school was a wide yellow stripe on the blacktop, painted-green chain fences, and fireplugs brushed the color of maraschino cherries—I imagine *upkeep* must have been an important grown-ups' word.

But there was a glass-strewn side road, too, that I knew; a cousin to the main ways. It took you to Jungletown. It slinkyassed and did the bebop and conked you out when you weren't looking. This street did the nasties. It shimmyshook its sugargoods. It pissed in the crannies. It cursed. It was always in heat, and gave that crease-rich musky reek. It juked, it conned you with a rouged-on grin, it winked and it sassed, it knew the score, it rigged the score, it wore great dimestore diamonds in its teeth and had a knot of blues forever turning painfully but praline-sweet in its throat-phlegms.

By the time I was bar-mitzvah age, the street girls I'd seen there peripherally, the glanced-at blues-band bars and peeked-at ribs shacks, were a murky, frightening, very real calling away from the suzerainty of matched place-setting citizenship. And even at seven I understood that families, no matter how acceptably proper their major figures were, each had one tumbledown fray-edged cousin of mysterious making-do. For me, it was Cousin Vi—she was, what?, maybe thirty. Her story is this story; if you keep on reading you'll meet her again. Who left and returned. Her smoky voice. Her eyes that twitched but Knew Things.

Now I know the folks of Jungletown considered it a native place, their home, and no Exotica or Elsewhere, just the breakfast bacon x-spot that they woke to every day. But back then, it was my Heaven and Hell. Its sexy seraphettes and pimp-mobile lucifers were all I required for imagery of what a person needed most to pray for and to fear—though no one else I knew seemed to think of that road and its denizens much at all; or, if they did, they never mentioned it as anything emblematic of Another World Completely.

There's a vaguely curious "pen drawing from the margin of a twelfth-century psalter" reproduced in James Burke's book *The Day the Universe Changed,* and an even more curious caption to it. "Women are shown shearing sheep," we're told, "spinning the wool into thread, and weaving it into rough, broadweave cloth on a medieval vertical loom. The threads are held in position by a weight at the bottom of the frame." Well, yes. And this is all we're told. The picture illustrates a specific medieval technology in action.

But the fleeciness this process has shorn from the backs of the sheep is given to the ground: it rises underfoot in billowy loaves, like clouds. One woman kneels at the loom and plays her hands across its strings in the pose of a harpist. Another woman is positioned just in front of two wide splays of wool that are stretched as if for some stage like being combed or stored for spooling, and these are actually attenuating graceful swoops burst forth from either shoulder: she has wings. As much as we're touring the bleating and knuckle-skinned details of village industry, we're touring Heaven itself.

And Hell—below the billows, populating a balancing, basement register, are human figures being lanced through hand or chest by shaggy-fleshed creatures, tailed and sort of rooster-crowned in inky spikes. The three-headed Hound of Hell is on guard. Stylized flames, like spear points doing hula, set the scene. It makes a punning sense: we know wool must be *carded,* and my dictionary says "to card" is also "to torture by drawing a wool card over the bare back or other part of the body."

Of all this, Burke says nothing. He's on a street of the world where textiles warp and woof. But there are Two Worlds—always. Two Worlds.

After Sunday school the sky was always a little more open to sentinel Pillars of Fire and Flaming Chariots and Ancestral Presence. Baby Moses was aided by angels, one to the left, and one to the right, like parentheses. Ezekiel saw a Wheel of Eyes. A rainbow was God's signing the dotted line of His contract with humankind . . .

Let's say I'm seven. It's night. Outside, a pearly mist is rising from the black earth into black sky. It's like . . .

Always, the spiritual happens for us in the metaphors of what's solid.

. . . it's like white slips being lifted over the ready black breasts of Jungletown.

It's chalk on a blackboard—there, then erased. Albumin . . . Vanilla . . . Miasma . . .

I'm seven, I'm droopy, the constellations are drinking their glasses of warm milk off of the planet, and now I can go to sleep.

2.

She married a doctor. All of the other cousins did well enough — a by-the-hour electrician, a shoe store manager near where the mega-rent complex of office buildings went up, the entrepreneur of a wholesale cantaloupes chain, that kind of thing. One drank (I won't say which), but none was a bum or played the ponies. Still, this was different. She married a *doctor,* a specialist — the heart! For us, back then, you may as well have said her plucky spaceship had berthed on another planet altogether. "And" — as if that weren't enough of radiant luck in one life, this is the statement my family always added — "he loves her." Imagine! "A surgeon!" "He *dotes* on her."

Well so did I. I watched each lanky llama-shank jiggle of hers across a room as if she puppeteered the cosmos by her movements. She had a spring somewhere in her pelvis — no one walked the way she did. At seven I could understand, just short of having words, why someone thirty-seven wanted her up close. "A *doctor* . . . !" "Listen, they have a maid. Who does All The Cooking! Three days a week she comes. A maid! Do you *believe* it?" And when I slept over — for Cousin Vi liked me back, and "can't have children," and so we both owned reasons for thinking such weekends a treat — it was a snap to patter from bed to the bathroom (nouveau austere — she'd moved a taste-step away from my mother's flocked, fluffed, goldspecked gewgaw decor) and place my cheek in the multifoliate soilage of the linen basket, basking in that salmony silky salad of her lingerie and its heady inexplicable bouquet.

Though it wasn't just sex. She'd truly *listen* to me, not through me. And when she was alone in a corner — often she'd go alone to a corner — lavender veils closed over her eyes, at least that's how I thought of it, "her little trances" Leonard would say, and she'd do what I longed to do at family holiday convenings but couldn't "get away with," raying herself to the *doppelgalaxy* Vi II, only her pretty husk here.

Where others tried to teach me that Judaism was one enormous thorny grid of prohibitions and guilts, she told me stories of the Baal Shem Tov — who flew to Heaven, to plead for his people;

who wrestled the Devil's sorcerer ghouls; who parleyed as one with the field vole and the cart pony and the shrike; who prayed by dancing, then slept with the sweat dried over his body like plates of armor . . . All this, she told me. And when she disappeared I felt abandoned, I'd bet, in my own understanding of being bereft, as much as Leonard. "What can I say?" he'd say. He'd spread his hands, charading emptiness. "Gone. One morning, no warning, gone."

The dumb things we remember! — my mother, weeping mascara into her coffee, then drinking it in a daze. For me, that meant the world was wobbling on its axis, it was kin to gravity failing. Thirty-three years now, and I still see her eyes unraveling that way.

They thought violence at first, of course. A policeman awkwardly asked me some questions. In an otherwise event-impoverished family, Vi's vanishing screamed like blood on snow. Except there was no blood, there were no clues of any kind, and after weeks a private detective was hired, and after months a letter arrived in any case.

She was living now on the coast. Yes, she was alright; no, nobody made her do it; she loved us all, goodbye. By now it's hard for me to know what I remember from being seven — only very few of these scenes are stained in something so indelible as my mother's grief-mascara — and what I've patched together later. Usually, I was shooshed from the room. One quick vignette: my Cousin Norman shrugging, "Yaah, she's crazy," and Cousin Lottie biting the air at him, "Hush!" And one other, the clearest, perhaps because of my terror: my mother refolding a letter (*the* letter? I don't know) and she's wailing, "A butcher's assistant!" over and over, "A butcher's assistant!" — like that. Then, as if unsure whether to whisper it, for secrecy, or shout it with the thousand mouths she was clenching inside her, that needed to shout — ". . . and not even *kosher!*" It comes out just a hoarse sob. Then someone notices me and shooshes me off to bed. That night I saw her: She packed her bags — if she had bags. She scrammed. She vamoosed. She walked out into the blotter-blue night like a fountain-pen word. It was her name, and by morning the new white sky was clean of it.

Because her voluntarily leaving her upscale life was unthinkable, nobody thought about it. (Kidnappers would have been better.) It never happened, she never was. Leonard donated time to a transients' clinic and joined the Yankovs' every-other-Wednesday poker club. My months whirled like the color wheel in art class, into one continuous blur. Mad Mario drummed with two red pencils at the back of my head in class, he was the size of a suckling rhinoceros and I hated him. He was—oh, like something unstuck from a deep-fat fryer. Each month my Disney comic book arrived by mail: Mickey solved "The Riddle of The Disappearing Railroad" (a serial—three issues), giving Goofy many a sidekick's chance for scratching his bony noggin and, in wonder, muttering Dr. Watson-like, "Gawrsh!" There was a vile child murder, parts discovered floating the lake in oil drums, for weeks it kept me sleepless. That was the spring I first collected fireflies; asinine labor, I later decided and, anyway, somebody lied: you could *not* read by the collective blips of a jar of them in a dark room. Nor, it turned out, could you train a box of ants to spell out HELP like people in old cartoons on desert islands seen from rescue planes. I don't know who thought up that stupid idea. Pacey, probably. Yeah or maybe Barton. We found a turtle; it died. They really do snap. Its back was a map of green cobbles. Winter was bitter and summer was hellish—that's what life in Chicago's about. One autumn day my mother said "Dress nice, be good, she's coming back home," and I knew who.

3.

This is when the Baal Shem Tov was young himself, almost as young as the children. (But "Baal Shem Tov" is a title of honor, it shines on a man invisibly, like the crown a crown would wear.) At this time, the boy was called Israel.

His father, Rabbi Eleazer, explained this when the boy was five, he told him, "Israel, listen, one of the Innocent Souls of Heaven lives in you—though you may seem a poor shack for its dwelling, in the world's eyes. Use your specialness well and do not fear the Enemy." Then he died. The boy's small wails, his first, flew straightway to the Gates of Heaven unescorted by any of the Mediary Angels all cries need. And so God saw then, the child had the power worthy of being Baal Shem Tov, God saw this and took note. And so did the Enemy.

Israel lived in the woods, in a cave there, in a nest he fashioned of moss. All day he sang for joy of being alive and able to sing at all, he spoke with the lynx (who sheathed her claws for him) and the jay and the bear and the mudfish burrowed in backwards up to her gills like a scoop in the pea-mash barrel, he could read their droppings like the *aleph-beth,* and at night, by the moon, he watched the weaving stream froth at its edges like a prayer shawl fringed in silk.

Now he was ten. He left his nest in the hills, he strode down to the village Horodenka. Here, he became the *melammed's*—the schoolteacher's—helper. It was Israel's duty to visit the houses just past sunrise, wake the children, and lead them to *cheder*—to school—in a careful line. "Hasten! Hasten! Time for study!"—these were his instructions. In the evening he was to lead them back home.

Well this was the eighteenth century. In Eastern Europe, in Jewish village life, the Application of a Mind to Learning was paramount, the poorest of parents went crustless at the supper hour for books. The first time a child was taken to *cheder*, this was the ritual: he was wrapped up in a prayer shawl like a scroll. They believed in the text, and they were serious, these Jews. All day and into the night to the next day, they could parse their explications of a sage's commentaries ever finer, word by word, to airborne filaments of thought—but a pun was beyond them. Not one window knew a flower pot. They spoke in hushes and scratchy funereal keens. By day they worked the turns of the fields until their hands were red; by night they labored unstintingly at the lines of books until their eyes were redder.

And in this community, Israel taught his dour young charges to sing. Instead of heading straight for the thatchy *cheder,* and out of no programmatics but simply from out of the tympani in the wrist-pulse, Israel sang "Praised be His holy name, amen!" in a loopy route through pastures still meringued with early mist, and his students sang too. The village took note; now adults, even, hummed sometimes as they coopered a barrel. God on High took note; such singing honored the quick of Creation. And the Enemy, Satan, took note.

(Was it here that she paused for effect? I think so. And her eyes twitched with such a histrionic mock-terror!)

This is the first extended narrative in the canon of tales concerning the Baal Shem Tov, the first of many that (like any hagiography) work backwards to a sect's peculiar characteristics' founding gesture: joy, in this case — worshiping the Lord through celebration. I've seen Hassidic Jews, black-coated, gender-segregated, clannish in the streets, and it's been difficult to think of them as festive. But I was a foreigner (though a Jew myself) and so perhaps not privy to open display, or not open myself to its nuance. In any case, I can only trust the lucid beauty the origin story held for me when I was seven, and she was willing to meet my being seven, and the Evil One Himself was conjured into the room.

Now the Enemy cannot work his damage directly; he requires his many ambassadors. But not one creature — fox or snake or needle-bearing bee — would turn against Israel. The Enemy stormed. (The sky stormed.) And by lightning-flash the Enemy saw a simpleminded charcoal burner, an old man, in his hut, asleep. The Enemy plucked out his soul — as easy as gutting a chicken, *ssp!* And he replaced it with a Dark Seed. When the clouds thinned and the dawn sun peeked out painfully naked, the old man was a wolf, an actual wolf, but worse than a wolf. And he wanted the children.

He stalked them. He was their shadow, their pre-hearse, nothing shook him off the blood-scent, and the noise he made was like cats being boiled. The littlest children fell spasming in fright. "Stay here" — and Israel, who was ten, approached the wolf thing, oh he was like a small boy walking toward a great hill, and his arms were extended palms out and the Name of God was on his lips, and Israel entered the wolf — like walking into filthy water, you cringe but still it's just water, he waded completely, atomically, into the being of the wolf.

He passed through jaws that were like the stake fence of the graveyard. Inside, dark performed for him like light in the Outside World, he could see. The spine ran overhead, the ribs along it like white bats stretching in sleep. He saw the bones, he could have polished them like chalices and beakers, he saw the fatty candles the body keeps burning or else it dies. And he saw his own face in the oily sheen of the pericardium. Israel touched the heart—but gently, it was like feeling the open softspot hole of a newborn's skull. Then Israel reached inside and took the Dark Seed in his hand and jerked, once, hard.

The moan of the wolf they heard in the capital. (It was the Enemy moaning.) Israel walked back out and broke the Seed in two and the wolf toppled dead—a rug, a flea-run rug—in the grasses. And after that, though the Enemy plotted, though often the Enemy plotted and won and mourning wails broke from Israel's people . . . singing had come to the Jews, and dancing too. They came, they wouldn't leave. "For how can you worship the Lord who made the golden sun," inquired the Baal Shem Tov, "if first the yolk of the egg cannot make you giddy?" Remember, though: he *toiled* for his happiness, almost to fainting, his dance steps were apprenticed on the belly-floor of the wolf.

And this, said Cousin Vi, was his Preparing.

* * * *

Everywhere, that's the Preparing.

"A shaman's initiation comes when he is able to look the rainbow snake full in its glaring eyes as it swallows him"—Francis Huxley, in a chapter titled "The Way of the Other Body."

Mircea Eliade laves details: "The postulant remains in the Serpent's belly for an indefinite time. Finally the medicine men bring two kangaroo rats as an offering, whereupon the Serpent ejects the postulant, throwing him high into the air, [now] reduced to the size of an infant. . . . In short, the candidate becomes a medicine man through a ritual of initiatory death, followed by a resurrection to a new and superhuman condition." In the Vatican Etruscan collection, one vase shows us Jason at the end of his adventures being spewed—limp, damp, a chrysalis—from a serpent's gagging jaws.

The nameless heroine "Little Red-Cap" tumbles alive from the same transitionary gut ("How frightened I have been! How dark it was inside the wolf!")—and ever after, freedom is vouchsafed her: in the Hunt/Stern version of Grimm, the girl "went joyously home, and no one ever did anything to harm her again." A great, earned gift. The glow of extracorporeal knowledge must have seemed, for the rest of her days, to radiate from that scarlet cowl.

Or it might be an ambushing crocodile, a scorpion monster, a mantis queen—but the point is, it's an Entry Maw, and an Adept successfully exits. There's the tale of a Zulu woman swallowed by an elephant, and luggaged away in its stomach "she saw large forests and great rivers, and many high lands; on one side there were many rocks; and there were many people who had built their village there; and many dogs and many cattle; all was there inside the elephant." As for Longfellow's Iroquois patriarch-hero:

> Mishe-Nahma, King of Fishes,
> In his wrath he darted upward,
> Flashing leaped into the sunshine,
> Opened his great jaws and swallowed
> Both canoe and Hiawatha.

Raven, trickster-hero of the Eskimo of Bering Strait, insinuates himself down the throat of a whale-cow. He finds himself in a beautiful chamber, tended by a beautiful woman (Inua, the soul of the whale) and lighted beautifully by a lamp, the oil of which drips from a tube of living tissue that stems straight from the living lotiony whale-cow meat.

"Worldwide"—so Joseph Campbell calls the image.

Here's a photograph: I'm seven, it's near Thanksgiving, and Disney's *Pinocchio* is in re-release. Collodi's original novel has its (much more brutal) charm but isn't as seamless and svelte as the Disney. In Collodi, Pinocchio's accidentally gulped by "the terrible Dog-Fish," one mile long, and in its gut is reunited with his carver/father Gepetto; together, they simply walk from the fish's enormous mouth while it's asleep. In Disney's version, Pinocchio's searching for his father, and *intentionally* seeks out the whale called Monstro. And that scene—! The vastly corrugated, shadowed Gothic vaulting that's the roof of the whale's mouth . . . !

Their plan, you'll remember, is not only absolute brio (creating a fire from shipwreck flotsam, they're shot from Monstro's gullet in a massive gastric wave) but is intuitively keeping faith with myth: it's by the rubbing of his fire sticks that Raven forces disgorging . . .

I'm seven here. It's near Thanksgiving, and Disney's *Pinocchio* is in re-release, and Cousin Vi is back now after being swallowed up ten months in strangeness and "she'll be over tomorrow for turkey, pretend like nothing's happened." You can see my face beam with it all. It's the only photo I have of my several years in Sunday school, and what was the occasion for their grouping us, eight girls, three boys, in soldierly rows, I don't remember and can't guess.

And I can't remember my teacher's name, though her slightly doughy good looks make me sad now. One of the other boys is dressed in a shirt that's crammed with an all-over print of cowpokes wearing pinto chaps and whirling perfect infinity-signs in the air with their lassos. The Hebrew alphabet, of course, is tacked to the wall. One girl — Bess Samuels, I think — is showing a snowy flash of her panties — on purpose, you can tell by the foxfire in her eyes. And pinned to the bulletin board, just large enough to discern, is Jonah being heaved up.

— Not unlike the version I've found reproduced from a Bible from 1471: popped out like a jack-in-the-box, that sudden and neat, and his arms are upspread as if daylight were a basket of darkness that's just been laundered, so clean it's unseeable, and placed on his head to carry.

* * * *

Joseph Campbell: "That is why the approaches to temples are flanked by colossal gargoyles: dragons, lions, winged bulls. These are the threshold guardians, corresponding to the two rows of teeth of the whale."

Well that's the Big Picture. That's the Comparative Folklore and Ethnographic Survey Picture. I like it. You like it. For one thing, it's as misty as a riverbank by Turner — all those jagged-jawed voracious creatures blend, become a theory of voraciousness. It hovers in the air.

But we have to remember a picture so small it might be fitted in the locket that this grandmama still wears about her nearly dew-lapped neck. She was a young girl once, oh yes she was. Her hair a fine corn-tassel gold. So delicious. A wolf ate her up, oh yes. That's her. For an hour she walked through its veiny swamp, and organs she's never known in her husband, her three generations of children, herself . . . she cupped in her palm and held to her cheek and licked for the sheer salt salute of her tongue.

* * * *

and lived happily / the rest of her days / ever after / and none was so happy as / and lived / for the rest / ever after / and now the constellations / of her days / are drinking their glasses of warm milk / once / and lived / I'm seven / upon a time / lived happily ever after / happily ever after / and now I can sleep

* * * *

But a child's head, limbs, torso were found, in oil drums, in the lake. No, not one child—two kids, sisters. The Grimes Sisters. If I want, I can remember the size of the headlines. They were the size of the night. I could float through any one black letter screaming there and nobody hear me till dawn. And these two sisters, now, will never join the crazy Carpathian conga line of children praising the goodness of all Creation, no, and where is the Baal Shem Tov, perhaps we each need being a Baal Shem Tov, a lower case, littler, baal shem tov, a savior-and-flock in one, the paper thuds against the door every morning, the lake always forces some secret to shore.

4.
I think it was because she'd married a surgeon.

She watched the maid run rags up chair legs and — the only ribs she'd ever seen — venetian blinds; while he was marrow-intimate with hundreds of strangers' bodies.

Maybe that. Although probably more than that. What did *I* know? I was seven. I wanted to say some *something* so mean to Bess Samuels, she'd notice me, and I didn't know why I wanted that though it filled my head like a sparkling pile of emery.

So I wasn't a very astute observer. Mostly, it's a jumble of a dozen of us pretending nothing's unusual. My mother's made her standard — deviled eggs — to kick things off. Cousin Joey, the Cantaloupe King (this is true: he appeared on local TV in a chintzy foil coronet-and-scepter getup, copping appreciative feels of first-class melon representatives) is extolling the splendors awaiting us for dessert, then schleps out the clunker we've heard about a thousand times: Knock knock. / Who's there? / Cantaloupe. / Cantaloupe who? We chorus the punchline wearily: Cantaloupe tonight, the ladder's busted. Myra's complaining — money, backache, whatever; a "colored" insulted her on the bus; her nerve is pinched but the doctor, no offense Leonard, the doctor thinks he's God and says her muscle is sprained; a poodle at Bank and Eleventh went for her throat, a killer, it should be hauled away and shot, thank the Lord it was on a leash . . . And Leonard, too nervous to fake the mundane, is cheering my mother on, with invisible pompoms of inspiration, while she exasperatedly transfers the turkey from basting pan to silver serving platter . . .

And Vi stands up then as if in a trance. She's been playing the game with us, that no one ran away, nowhere, no time, and isn't it lovely weather so far this year. The game called Everything's The Same. And in a way, it is, and will be — nothing dramatic, I'm sorry, happens from this point on. She'll live contentedly with Leonard until he dies in 1983 of a heart attack — a "perfect couple," lubed in true attunement — and then she'll live with her adopted daughter Marlene and son-in-law Walt; she still does; on Evergreen Avenue. Everything hunky-dory.

Except for this moment. A stitch drops out of time. She rises, preternatural on my mother's wall-to-wall avocado-green carpeting, and glides to the turkey with absolute possessorship, and as if she's done this dozens of times before (but nobody's ever seen her even *in* a kitchen, not Vi-of-the-famous-maid-service, not dreamy Vi . . .) she plies the fork and carving knife with meister-pianist dexterity, and commandingly, fluidly, severs what needs to be severed, slivers and slabs, then finally stands behind her accomplishment with something like the look of matriculation upon her. It's shocking—I might as well have been watching one of the Grimes Sisters being dismembered—shocking because I recall, I recall (am I the only one?) my mother's suffering wail: "a butcher's assistant!" and all of the ten-month mystery we've so smoothly ignored comes crashing to the carpet like a felled steer onto an abattoir floor.

* * * *

Sawdust is best for sopping up the blood that gouts, sometimes to the width of a trouser-leg, from their throats.

So once a week Menachem, whose business was almost always in trade instead of money, delivered in person a goat-cart's worth of sawdust from his workshed's corners. And in return he'd leave with a bundle of that day's greasier trimmings, all that Israel could spare, which the dog loved dearly, and the rest he would mash to a grease he cleaned his tools with. Israel knew: this kept a balance, oh a tiny one but a balance nonetheless, in the larger Balance of the Glory of God that shines from each of His creatures, even the least of them, as the firefly is eloquent reminder . . .

When we hear the canon tales of the Baal Shem Tov in meaningful and chronological order, we learn eventually of his visits to Heaven Itself. He saw the Throne of Deific Radiance, he spoke with The Shimmering Hosts. But first, he needed to learn the details of this material world, to every tassel of capillaries reddening a tired eye, to the sheen of a single poppyseed. By now he had a wife. Near the village of Zahbie he worked as a lime-burner. For a while, a *shochet's*—a kosher butcher's—assistant.

In my favorite of the earthly adventures, there is a village magistrate with wizardly powers — the Evil One has bestowed these upon him in payment for certain wickedness — and with these he conjures an Absolute Moment of Agony for the Jews within his provenance (some sicken, pain is a bedmate, crops are spoiling . . .) and Time will halt at this Absolute Moment for these Jews, they'll live with no relief inside this Moment forevermore, unless (and this is the magico-contractual term that must be met) they sacrifice up to him their firstborn, "sacrifice by slitting the neck of their firstborn" (these are the words of the spell exactly), and deliver the yet-warm corpses in a pile to the City Gates by dawn.

(You see? It reverses the story of Abraham and Isaac in so many nefarious ways. Not to mention — and this was the stagey implication of Vi's macabre performance of the story — *what did they want with those fresh young corpses?*) The Baal Shem Tov can attempt to battle this wizard, but even he cannot undo the need for fulfilling a contract that's woven satanically of the Units of the Universe and sealed thereby.

You get through all that mumbojumbo embellishment, here's the moving part: one aged Jew, it could be Menachem's father, turning and turning in bed, and his own bones beating him painfully, the way a bully would beat a weary dog, but from inside. We need to see this now. For as the Baal Shem Tov has said, "The sky cannot be so huge for us we miss the lice on a hawk's wing" (only I think it sounds less sappy in the phlegm-and-clucking gutturals of the original).

And the good part: now the Baal Shem Tov dispatches his Spirit Self to contend with the wizard — into the skin of the bubble of Halted Time he sends it, and in that shimmering extradimensional arena, they battle: circles of fire, hellhounds, sudden crushing weight, you-name-it: I'll spare you the details. And his Bodily Self he sends among his people, offering counsel.

This is how it turns out: he wins the warlockian battle. And the City Guards discover at the Gates that morning a pile of freshly (and kosherly — that's the Bronx cheer gesture) slaughtered barnyard animals, steers mainly, in a stinking mess — all of them the firstborn of that season, thus the contract technically met. For the

Bodily Self had given the villagers rabbinic savvy (and sanction) in kosher ritual. A hand on their shoulders. A Baal Shem Tovly word. Then the knife to the jugulars of those creatures. Then dragging their hundreds of pounds. "For God Above will aid us if our labor fails. But first we must labor." —Or words to that encouraging and gurulike effect.

Menachem's father, in the workshed. Putting his shoulder into his awl. A lovely wheatcolor spiral of wood is bladed into the world, so thin, like the film on a soup. Outside, a hawk. Its spiral down the morning light. Lice. Hemoglobin. A lozenge of light on the floor, and a helix of sawdust (almost as if the air were pared and this was its rind) is miniscule1y, definitely, rising.

* * * *

No—now I remember. It was every *tenth* firstborn the magistrate demanded. A horrible tithing. I remember because I was hearing the word for the first time. She explained it. A tenth-share. Tithing. And I'm running around her in circles babbling *tithing tithing tithing* . . .

I'm her favorite. Me, she smoothly unfastens a sumptuous turkey drumstick for, presenting it to my goggle-eyed stare with the over-a-forearm flourish of a wine steward proudly offering the evening's best label.

Now she's grabbed the other leg. —Maracas! She and I, around the table, shaking out a carnival beat, for a moment only, nuts and together and somewhere else. "You're both insane"—Cousin Maxie, although said warmly enough. When she and I compose ourselves, resuming place and propriety at the table, her spell (and everyone's reaction-spell) is broken; easy familial gripe-and-gossip resumes; and that night and, so far as I can tell, the next thirty years for her and for most of us, flow circumspectly, routinely, and predictably ahead.

We'll meet each year for Thanksgiving. Like Uncle Noshie's hank of hair he combs across his bald spot—we make a little a lot. We eat. We gab. Each new Thanksgiving, That Other Thanksgiving grows—for a few of us—legendary. Grows—for the rest (not grows: diminishes)—out of history altogether.

* * * *

One time I put my ear to the door.

I don't know what I expected to hear. I didn't understand what I finally did hear, didn't understand exactly, although the timbre of Grown-Ups' Conversation, some nonverbal moiety of the accurate, always does flow through the various semipermeable membranes in a house.

Uncle Lem was opining. Vi had run off to California and been a whore. She walked the streets, turned tricks, she sold the pelvic whammy to pay her grocery bill. He didn't use those words, of course — he may have said "painted lady" or "lady of the night" or used the Yiddish for it, *nahfkie* — but somehow I understood, at least implicitly and, years later, in retrospect (I'll tell you all about it soon) the understanding drove home with explicitness. *Whore.* If she was, for that while, so be it.

But there were other opinions too, and Cousin Becka swore she had it on good but undisclosable authority that Vi worked (on the streets again this time, but) as an aide for a Salvation Army-type organization, easing the rotgut-scented night moans of the homeless. "You have to be a saint to do that."

If she was a saint, so be it. For the purposes of the story, the story called Going-Over-the-Threshold-and-Returning, it's all the same. Joseph Campbell: "The disappearance corresponds to the passing of a worshipper into a temple — where he is to be quickened by the recollection of who and what he is . . . The temple interior, the belly of the whale, and the heavenly land beyond, above, and below the confines of the world, are one and the same" — all "denoting, in picture language, the life-centering, life-renewing act."

By day, the yokel Israel was in charge of bucketing cattle's terror-shit.

* * * *

By night, the Baal Shem Tov visited Heaven. Meyer Levin, in *Classic Hassidic Tales:* "During the day, he served all living creatures. He took of his Power, and divided it among them. But at night his soul took freedom. She would no longer remain among the suffering. She took off time and space as two imprisoning fetters, and raised herself to the borders. She shook off the earth from her foot. She tried her wings. And the Heavens received her."

This is what his wife saw: the constellations drinking their glass of warm milk — up, up! A very faint radiance in the air, about his size and shape, and then it was gone — ascended. Whenever this happened, she kissed his eyelids — she kissed the eyelids of what remained. The *what* always remained. But the *who* was in Ultra-existence, arguing exquisite sausagecasing-thin delineations of Scripture with the rabbis and prophets of yore.

And there are stories: Barrister-wise, he argued his people's case when the Enemy had been granted license to savage the Jews. He searched for the souls of two sweet pious lovers death had sundered before the marriage day, and he wedded them in the Afterlife, the hand of an Archangel was the traditional wedding canopy, the *chuppah,* over their heads.

Etc.

But mostly, his Essence just roamed. He took part in no narrative, he didn't go adventuring. He simply was content to walk between the lines of the Torah — between the Original Urges behind these lines — as men on Earth walk canyons. He was part of the intracellular fluid of God's Thought, and the voltage of Genesis played like electrical lotion over his self here. Pulsars, quasars, gravity, phototropism — these are the gossip of angels, and he listened at the knotholes of Mystery's gates. He didn't "breathe," there wasn't "air" here, but the stuffs of the Glory of God rushed in what one could only call his "lungs" like an intubation. But, there weren't lungs; he was an Essence, he knew the Unutterable Name, the farthest-flung congregations of Earth could read in pitch-black by the light that streamed forth from him, here.

In his straw bed, back home, Israel breathed. Evenly and deeply. There, a woman didn't call him Baal Shem Tov, no, she had other names, pet names, childish fond and sexual names, I'm sure, though neither history nor legend records them. She kept watch at the body that was the anchor for his Essence in Heaven, she'd bend sometimes and lightly kiss his eyelids, yes, and this was a message that traveled up such ur-ethereal anchorchain, reminding him that he was not Eternal yet, but the sour slip of vigil-keeping was on her tongue and waited for his tongue to sweeten its chemistry.

This is my favorite of all of the Heaven tales: once, the Path of All Things Together spoke to his Essence, it told him, "Halt! This is the Boundary of the Path. Beyond it, the Oneness begins." And it beseeched him, "Go no further, for across the Boundary there is no turning back. But say that you will sever your Tie to the Earth, and the Oneness will open, and take you."

And the Essence lifted its head. "I *will* sever—"

On Earth the woman cried his name, once. "Israel!" This cry flew to Heaven, it nested in his mouth, he couldn't finish his sentence, and then he turned around.

This is what she saw: it was like sand falling into the bottom of an hourglass, only glowing sand. It fell to the bed in the shape of a living man. And he opened his eyelids and whispered her name.

—

Meyer Levin: "That was the last time the Master wandered through Heaven."

—

Cantaloupe?

Well, Vi eloped. Tell Cousin Minnie *that,* with her on-sale blender, her fuzzy fuchsia bargain-table house slippers, her dieting pills. Cousin Vi eloped, with herself, she was her own groom and her own back window ladder. Oh I know, she returned. That's the story, remember? Going-Over-the-Threshold-and-Returning. But first she eloped. She was her own speedway convertible. She lowered the top, and the hand of an archangel ran through her hair (you see it? chestnut pennants in the wind) and so was she wedded.

* * * *

And she'll return in a moment, that woman in a medieval manuscript illustration I referred to before. It's a fourteenth-century legal code, the *Yoreh De'ah,* and this is the section describing the laws of *shehitah* (ritual slaughter) and *terefot* (ritually unclean). Held in a border of vine scrolls, putti, and courtiers, is a room with an uptilted brickwork floor. The slaughtering room of a noble's house, it looks like. Four men attend to those grisly strokes, to which the miniature size of the vignette and its jewel-like colors give a look of clockwork perfunctoriness and almost Swiss-like clockwork preciosity.

Two of them slice the throats of hanging fowl. One rocks his blade across the throat of an ox, as large around as a small dog. And the other (he's the one I mentioned earlier) is unlooping the gut of an already slaughtered ox, slit now and hanging by its hind legs, as if casually running a tickertape through his hands as it issues the news.

The brick is red. One shirt is red, and one man's headgear. The comb of the rooster is the severe red of a polyp of African coral. Its neck spouts paisleys of blood. And the hanging ox's innards are coil on coil of red, as if paint straight from a modern tube were used to stuff it, squiggle on squiggle, red to the reddest power, the red of the body laid bare.

In back, a woman peeks around a doorway. By her manner and coiffure, she seems to be at home: the lady of the house, I imagine we'd call her. And yet she hasn't walked forthrightly into the room, to check (as is her due) on the labor in her domain. This may be proscriptively men's work, or rabbinic work, and her being there disallowed. And you can tell, a sort of hesitancy, a short-term flutter, informs her looking in. As I said: she'll return in a moment, that woman. Back to a room of green tile, and cool blue drapery.

Yes, but this *is* the moment. She's seeing The Other World.

* * * *

* * * *

5.

Heaven (*Merkabah,* the sphere of the Throne of God) is, to the school of Jewish mystics *Yorde Merkabah*, attained after only successful completion of a regimen of specific ascetic acts. "He must fast a number of days," Gershom G. Scholem writes about the initiate, "and lay his head between his knees and whisper many hymns and songs"—the standard self-oblivion of shamanic deprivation. "Finally, after such preparations, and in a state of ecstasy, the adept begins his mystical ascent."

There are seven levels to Heaven, and each has its guardian archon, and the soul requires a magic seal, certified with a secret name, to rout the hostile angels of each new level. There are manifold dangers. Doniel and Katspiel are the guardian archons of level six, and here, if the aspirant's soul mistakes the glittering marble plates of the palace of level six for water, for "hundreds of thousands and millions of waves of water" (evidently a common misapprehension among ascending souls), the angels "will strike his head with iron bars." For one whose perseverance, purity, and "chosenness" are adequate, however, the series of trials is more than compensated for: a vision of the Throne of the Creator, at the Topmost Level Imaginable, ringed by pillars of flame.

Curiously—and we don't know why—this visionary journey of the soul to heaven is always termed "the descent to the Merkabah." It's what *Yorde Merkabah* means—"the descenders." "The paradoxical nature of this term is all the more remarkable because the detailed description of the mystical process nonetheless consistently employs the metaphor of ascent and not of descent."

We don't know why, and yet we do. There is no "up" or "down" in outer space, and outer space is theophany's point-of-view. Francis Huxley supplies this anecdote: "A German missionary among the Berg Damaras of Africa was once told that the dead inhabit little huts in the sky and that these huts were also the mounds in which their bodies were buried. He asked how this could possibly be so. 'You are separating the two ideas in your mind too much,' he was told by an old Damara. 'With us, it all coincides.'"

When Raven returns, bowel-smeared and blubber-epauletted, gastrus-slimed, from the belly of the whale, and brings his people the knowledge of fire sticks, he brings the same enabling fire Prometheus does, after making his superlunary trek to the cloudcarpet halls of the gods. We see that *animal,* the whale, and *animus,* the soul, are hinge-wings flying the psychic fundament in tandem. There are moving stairs that "escalate" and moving rooms that "elevate," but every day they bear as many people down as up. The threshold knows: the only direction worth more than half-a-gnat's-ass is *in.*

And so Muhammed ascends through a series of seven heavenly gates (at each, its cheerful greeters) and then, at last, to "the divine throne." A Mithraic initiate wills himself up a seven-runged "planetary ladder from darkness to light." Inanna, that sexy, sure, and prototypical Sumerian goddess, she who was "Queen of Heaven," she "abandoned heaven, abandoned earth, to the nether world she descended," and at each of seven gates the portalkeeper of the Sumerian Hell removes another item of her authority or article of her dress until, at the seventh gate, "all the garments of ladyship of her body were removed." It's only then she may face Ereshkigal, her sister goddess, ruler of darkness and death.

They are, in a sense, the same one goddess in two opposing aspects. Zarathustra, Enoch, and St. Paul prophesy celestial spheres; Persephone, Orpheus, and Aeneas travel the underworld. These are all, in a sense, one seeker, and their aspects are united in Dante, who took both the high road and low.

Returned from Heaven, the Merkabah mystic presumably has been granted revelation of "the mysteries and wonderful secrets of the tissue on which the perfection of the world and its course depends, and the chain along which all the wings of the universe are connected, sewn together, and hung up." Aeneas returned from the underworld, where "all things were revealed to him: the destiny of souls, the destiny of Rome, and in what wise he might avoid or endure every burden."

Regal Aeneas, Her Highness Inanna, Trickster Raven: these figures are Kings or Queens or Knaves on face-cards: either side is top, is bottom.

When his wife looked at the body of the Baal Shem Tov, the body in bed while his Essence astral-projected, it was like looking at an egg being candled, luminous, and with that filamental vascular pulse; and then the filament was gone; and by morning returned; it had journeyed in distances only measurable by units of star hearts, trilobite tread, the lashing of sperm, the tailstreak of comets, dust's dance, dawnlight like the white keys a piano offers up and down (there is no "up" or "down") and coal the black keys . . .

And for we who can only be lowercase baal-shem-tovs-of-the-surface-moment, there's surface—and lateral—travel: the pilgrimage.

* * * *

In the hammerheaded desert sun of central Australia, Ayer's Rock—over a thousand feet tall—breaks from its baked land like the back of some gargantuan whale just about to breach.

This isn't whale country, though—that's my imposition. For the Pitjendara tribe, the Rock is a three-dimensional, enterable text of the First Ten Ancestors. These were the Man and the Woman and, no less important, the Liru snake, the Kunia snake, the willy-wagtail woman, the kingfisher woman, the sand mole, the hare wallaby, and two lizards. Each is a totem of one of the Pitjendara clans.

The Rock itself is scored, infolded, gullied, and caved, is lunar surface here and mazedly foliaged there. The Ancestors' history is written in these natural features. Grass in some of the cracks is the pubic muff of the hare-wallaby women; certain small rocks are their children. Small caves are the nostrils through which a hare-wallaby man lanced his nose-bone. Four boulders are the children of the willy-wagtail woman, and a white mark is their urine. There are many dozens of meaning-bountiful sites like these—the living, monumental proof of mythological narrative.

The various clans perform their various rites at their pertinent sites on the Rock. Novices being initiated into clan adulthood are taken in turn to each momentous place. In certain caves they cut the veins of their arms and let blood spurt across the wall. "Sticks may be thrown at such and such a rock where a mythical event occurred, a salutation made at another" — Francis Huxley. "This is the equivalent of following the Stations of the Cross within a church, or of going on pilgrimage."

In Paris in the eleventh century, that approximately same endeavor would have meant congregating for Mass at L'Église de Saint Jacques, in preparation for lifting the pilgrim's walking-staff and starting the hike of 1,000 miles to Santiago de Compostela in northwest Spain. Uncounted thousands took the journey — criminals and nobles both. Some of them barefoot (the holiest method). Some of them adding chains or shackles (the better to punish the trespassing flesh). (The Count of Anjou, Fulk Nerra, walked to Jerusalem barefoot four times and, on the final occasion, had himself flogged and dragged to Christ's tomb by a horse.)

For even the least masochistic or needy-of-expiation, the journey was arduous: a shaman's initiatory tortures, it's tempting to term it, plotted (and plodded) along a linear graph. The plains about Castile were malleted flat and chalk-dry by the sun. Below Bordeaux were boggy stretches of waist-deep mud and, once inside, the getting out was never sure. Some rivers were poisonous. The roads themselves were often little more than jerkied versions of highways — spindly, rock-strewn, bramble-battered things. And there were bandits, though the word perhaps has too romantic an air. They'd leave with human eyeballs threaded about their necks, still damp, and ass-blood crusting their cocks. But innkeepers, and pilgrims themselves, committed murder — D. J. Tice, in his essay "The Long Road to Heaven," calls it "appallingly common." And the say-so of the times was that wolves, bears, and wild boar lurked greedily, crazed for biped meat.

(I see the boy Israel telling his comrades "Shush!" then purposely walking from a cower-place in shadow, into the starkly revealing afternoon light, to stare at the wolf, to stare along the pinlit feral opticways, to take a first step into the grip of its otherness, to say the Name of Names in utmost confidence and stride straight into the alternate universe pullulating heart and swaggy chandeliers of wolf-fat, chanting, chanting . . . Thus do some walk into their uppercasehood. The Long Road to Heaven. The Baal Shem Tov.

Into the gut of the beast. The bowel, that spiral . . .)

* * * *

On certain medieval cathedral floors (the nave of Chartres is an example) we find elaborate labyrinth patterns inlaid. The function of the spiral is to compact, of course, and these remind us graphically that even a thousand miles of linearity can be woven around a single brief axis of moment or place. This is what happens to Raven, for instance: winding the critical density of the whale's bodycavitycoil maze. (The entrails: trails *in.*) The French cathedral labyrinths "were placed at the west end of the nave and people made a pilgrimage on their knees, following the pathway to the center, which is said to have been called *Sancta Ecclesia* or *Ciel*" (W. R. Lethaby).

The threshold — it can be broken, by some, just standing there. Consider Rosa Bonheur:

* * * *

at the slaughterer's. She's dressed as a man. She's fixing that picture, that diorama of blood and bone knob, texture-and-shade in her mind.

Rosa Bonheur, the artist. "One must know what is under their skin," she said. "Otherwise your animal will look like a mat rather than a tiger." And so she turned to the abattoirs. Of her quest there, M. du Pays said that "in Paris there are but few animals, only horses, dogs, and tomcats. The beef, cows, and sheep only enter the city in the form of *fillets, entrecôtes, et gigots.*"

It's 1850, say. A day when any fleck of char or wafting thread of green batiste is picked out in the air in perfect affirming silhouette. And Rosa Bonheur is leaning against a rail, widest eyes in the city, unmoving: studying the filets.

Having attracted overmuch of huffily admonishing attention in this "man's world" on earlier forays, she's come in scruffed-up incognito: "boyish" in figure, cropheaded, slight, it's easy enough to pass unnoticed in male trousers-and-smock. (By 1857, she'll have a police certificate granting her official permission to do just this.) So she can stand there. Stand there. And enter.

She needs to see the inner fittings and their greasy joint work, needs to see the parquetry of muscle, the ride of its slippage, its fibery weave. Now a butcher and his assistant are paying out the guts, hand over hand, like sailors piling mucused ship rope. The spiral. Standing there. Entering.

Now they're hoisting a carcass by rope, one of them pulling on either side. Formulaic in pose this way, they might be lifting a dazzlingly crimson version of the Tablets of the Law.

Such red! Precursor-red. It dominates the space. People are now no more than its minor amendments.

Standing there. Being elsewhere.

* * * *

And Cousin Vi said: "This is what happened after the death of the Baal Shem Tov.

"While he was alive, whenever he had a difficult task, he would take to the woods, and there light a fire, and mumble prayerful words, and so the task would be accomplished.

"After his death his successor the Maggid of Meseritz, faced with a similar problem, would take to the woods and say: we no longer know how to light such a fire, but we can mumble prayerful words. And so the task would be accomplished.

"A generation later Rabbi Moshe Leib of Sassov needed solving the problem, and said: we do not know how to light such a fire, or know what prayer to intone. But we know the place in the woods to sojourn to, and this must be sufficient. And it was sufficient.

"And yet another generation passed. Rabbi Israel of Rishin was beseeched to perform the task. And from his room he said: we cannot light the fire, we do not know the prayers, the place in the woods is a mystery to us—but we can tell the story of how it was done.

"And the story told well was enough."

* * * *

I live in Kansas now. I'm forty. In autumn here in Wichita the leaves are rouge and banana-yellow a while, then pile at bases of trees like doffed coffee lingerie still at the feet of the woman who's unfastened it all. Thanksgiving means Skyler and I were at the Sobins'—Theodora and Tony—with Don and Cindy, Phil and Kat, and Melissa stopped by, and Nicky is one year old and testing the world by goofily banging his forehead against it.

Children still die horribly in the newspapers, there are marriages I know whose bonds are being tested by some serrated blade or another, lucky people still snuggle anyway, everywhere there's going to be December nakedness over these trees, then their tentative, peekaboo, celadon chemises.

Do you know turkeys are so stupid they'll lift their heads in the rain for a drink and remain in that position and drown? No. Yes. Benjamin Franklin wanted the turkey named the national bird.

Etc. It was something in our dinner scene, I guess, that brought so much of Vi to mind. I even told the cantaloupe joke.

And something . . . Tony, a moment, his hands on the drumsticks, looking as if he were working the oars of an artifact dinghy over scale-model Atlantic waves . . .

Now we tell the stories, and they're enough, of the ones we call Pilgrims.

6.

Look at me: my cheek is waffled with asphalt burns. I'm pale and beet in wild alternation. My parents have called the doctor (as creaky and antique as a thrift-shop morris chair, he still makes house calls). "What happened?" But I won't talk. It's not because my tongue is swollen like a knockwurst, though my tongue *is* swollen. Say I'm sixteen. I'm jubilant. I've been to, and back from, Jungletown.

Why I went—you know. Because I was curious. Because it was there. Because the nineteenth century needed to detail-in each x and rill of Africa and Asia on their screechingly blank faced maps, and so did I. Because some sexual tomtom wouldn't shut up in my heart, because the server in my high school cafeteria bent low above her cumulus of institutional mashed potatoes and one unnerving shadow between her breasts would put the feel of a pat of butter into my balls all day. Because. Some idea of risk, of swagger. Some — you know. Some something. Because.

What happened there — none of your business. But I'll say this: I was right. It *did* shimmy like estrogen flan. It was sequins and rats' eyes and glints on a sax. It had big saucy smiles like pork ribs. It was righteous though it wasn't alright. The flimflam happened there, your nerves wore craziness like boutonnieres. It was nowhere for someone like me, though in the long run — and I ran, by the end — I acquitted myself with some minuscule earned dignity. In the blues riffs. In the nude ruffs of the dancers. In the eight-ball's clean geometry. In the dirty back cracks. Oh a lot happened there, and a lot of it was pleasure, and a lot of the pleasure in Jungletown is business — but it's none of your business, I'm sorry.

And I saw Bess Samuels there. I was on top of her, my money in her swingy beaded purse, before she recognized me from nine years before. I couldn't have recognized her. I mean I was so puke-scared — of any sash-slam in the cathouse, and of my own dickheaded decision-making as well — that I was seeing every tea-deep stain on the sheet and every strawberry mole on her body through a jelly-film of fear. But also . . . how much had I changed? I don't know. But she was a woman — at least a proto-woman — now, and not only the amazingly beckoning/formidable wet fur in between her thighs, but also a cache I sensed in her of brassy knowledge beyond me, though she'd started where I'd started from . . . well, it took me a while. She called herself Sunshine here. A white girl in a black block. With her jet hair, tipped a cheese-spread blonde.

But she recognized me, right off. And so I was right off her in a second, soft now, babbling. She kept the money anyway. That was okay with me. And until her pimp knocked that my time was up, and things got a little nuts, we reminisced. We talked about Sunday school while her colleagues around us sucked truckers.

I'm not saying the experience was good or bad or anything like that. I'm just saying I'm back home now, still frightened but surely not sorry, and with my new, few black-and-blue badges of pride. The doctor's on his way. He's coming from Hospital Street (we called it that). And I'm saying two thoughts that flashed through me then:

1. a picture of Vi in my head / a sudden understanding of the implications in Uncle Lem's curt, nasty accusation / he was dead by then, and Vi was some old lady (all of thirty-nine or so) I rarely thought of at all / *a whore*, he'd said / and a voice in me said calmly back: *so be it* / and
2. a vision of the Disney cartoon / he runs away, he undertakes adventures / by the end he's dancing around Gepetto's studio / the whale is history now / he's no one's puppet / he's / I remember I said these magic words out loud to myself / a *Real* Boy.

* * * *

Dear Fannie (and Everyone!)
Hello! A small bird sings each morning outside my window, it is gold and looks like the handguns here I see in the pawn shop windows. This is such a different world! I know it is strange to you, it must be, even to me it is, that this is where I live now. I am writing Leonard too, today, "the dear", so do not worry. How you all must be upset! Do you understand? In the pawn shop windows I see guitars that once made music as alive as my gold bird, they look like the bodies of children with large crying mouths—they are in these windows because their lives are ruined! There are so many more lives than we knew growing up! How is Albert, the sweet? And "everyone". Fannie, do you even know what a pawn shop is? And so I remembered your nickname when we were children together combing out the dolls hair, it was Faygeleh, yes it was, Jewish for "little bird." And then I knew I should write you.

Do not worry. You would if you knew how little I sleep. But I am on fire with seeing new things, and so I give out too much light for me to fall asleep in. I work at a clinic here, for the homeless. I see men and women every day with sores on their bodies oh they are the size of breakfast steaks! Do you believe me? One with maggots inside. It was a little girl, no more than seven yrs, I saw a red hole in her ribs crawl. It was like an eye. And so it is proper to stare back. These people must have healthy eyes stare back. And so you see I am not sick "in my head" I am healthy, that is why the doctors keep me working here so. The patients call the doctors butchers because of so much blood, and I am a butcher's assistant. And not even kosher! No one "gets" my little joke here, I know you will smile.

Also everything is fine. And I do wish you could walk on the coast with me! And Becka too, she always liked our small trips to the country so much and said Nature in capital letters. Hello to Becka! And to Everyone. The waves break, it is like seeing the white in an apple at your first bite. All the dark and then the bite of white. Do you know I saw whales? Yes! The high school could hold prom night in a whale! I was never asked to prom. I never really saw a sore on anybody until out here. I am scared sometimes that the shine on the sickness I see is as thrilling to me as the sun like a whole yolk frying lovely on the beach. But I can help the sickness! I lay my hands on its shine. I do not think there is water enough in all of the ocean to put out my fire.

So, you see, tell everyone I am fine. Do not come here. I love you. A "friend" took a picture of me, here it is. Not too like a movie queen! But, so? Fannie, please, there are whales! They will not fit in a garage. I hope you understand. Please give my love. Do you like the little doll I am holding, the girl seven yrs put it into my hands and now she is dead, I am going to name it for her. A grocery store is nearby and I have my old alarm clock.

Love,
Vi

* * * *

How would she have read it?—my mother, half-insane with grief. Or maybe I misunderstood—after all, I was seven. "A butcher's assistant!" Then all that wailing.

But things long vaulted away become unlocked when family members die. And so I finally saw Vi's letter. Not that it really made much clearer by then, or should have. It was *her* ten months of walking through the wolf, and I could always only be a child singing in line behind her.

And who was the "friend"? For a while the rich innuendo attending those very atmospheric quotation marks intrigued me. But I couldn't ask Vi—for her, those months were farther away than the days of the Baal Shem Tov. Then some time passed, and the intrigue did too. *So be it.*

And the picture? Here's the picture:

The doll's face is plain: a pie-eyed wedge-mouthed Raggedy Ann-type cuteness. But the way the camera's flash has glanced off Vi, she's all shadow-and-glowing. It's almost a strangely animal visage this has given her, elongating certain features, blunting others. Really she looks most like a sister to the figure in that medieval illustration I looked at so long ago: Ruth, gleaning. Ruth-with-the-animal-head. Ruth-with-the-extralife-knowledge.

And the first words, *"Every dollop says 'dybbuk' or 'God',"* in letters the size of garden gates, float eye-high through this picture.

7.

The murderer of the Grimes Sisters . . .? He or she was never caught. The Enemy is still at work, through us, his switchblades and his tongs.

Vi lives on Evergreen, a placid woman, graying gracefully into her mid-sixties. She's a grandmother now (she and Leonard adopted children; gradually, my place in her life, like a child's top, wobbled off-center and then stopped spinning). I see her on holidays. She sits them, a boy and girl, at her feet, and through their obvious itchiness she tells them the grand old stories. "This is when the Baal Shem Tov was young himself, almost as young as the children . . ."

The leaves are green. The leaves are red. I suppose, to a deity's vision, it changes as quickly as traffic lights. We must look like confetti—our lives—to the stones of the Earth. It's night, I watch the world outside be poured back into its ink bottle. Then it's morning: the sun is gilding the lamp post across the street like an incipit.

Cousin Vi returned so that the ordinary could continue. So

that each Thanksgiving the table would be set. That's finally everything: a molar gone, a nipple beading nacreously with milk, a mourning band worn on an arm the way the papers wear the black screams of their headlines . . . After Aeneas won his way into Hell, crossed the wretched River of the Dead, faced down the dread three-headed Guardian Dog of Hell, and was rewarded for his labors with a ghostly show of Infinity and marrow-rousing Wisdoms, then, says Joseph Campbell, "He returned through the ivory gate to his work in the world."

This, then, is the import of the planets-juggling, spirit-rendering, omphalos-connoitering travails of They Who Sojourn In The Wolf For The Rest Of Us: "Thus the next moment is permitted to come to pass."

Did Aeneas even remember? The Hassidic Jews have an anecdote: In the womb, the child learns the Holy Torah inside out, and is shown the secrets of the universe. But at birth an angel strikes it on the mouth; at that, all is forgotten.

Once, I came in from a long walk. It was only me—and the stars, those accent marks for wordless concepts. I sat down to a book of thirteenth- to fifteenth-century Hebrew manuscript illustrations. An angel there, the size of one sure stroke of ink, was speaking. It said:

Whenever we're here we're also somewhere else.
Including his breath, a man reaches to Jupiter.
A leaf is as deep as the sea: just ask pi-mesons.
Whoever we are we're also someone else.
Our very first possession is a shadow.
Light is only the language Time speaks to its children.
There's land, and then there's water, and then there's air:
beyond that . . . don't ask, go home.
Soap plates in the sink, make love, hang pictures.

* * * *

Skyler, once when you were asleep I kissed your eyelids—lightly, you didn't wake. The world kept turning, fondled by the sky like a lucky talisman. The bones of the dead remained in their casual schema in the planet—like the lines we imagine in between the stars. The dead could lead us to China and back this way. The travel of a single atom, out of the body, floating, into another body, a leaf, a lung . . . could lead us around the world and back, except we wouldn't be here by then. You woke. You said you dreamed a woman opened a sealed envelope. She understood how much it was filled with love, although it came from so far, the message itself was unreadable.

You were dreaming. You were The Other World's tithing.

I come into the bedroom, from writing this. It's my glass of warm milk, and now I can sleep.

I can sleep, having reached the day's threshold.

Author's Note: Most of my sources are cited in-text. Some books I particularly used or abused I would like to list, with thanks: Dore Ashton and Denise Browne Hare, *Rosa Bonheur, a life and a legend*; James Burke, *The Day the Universe Changed*; Joseph Campbell, *Hero With a Thousand Faces*; Mircea Eliade, *Occultism, Witchcraft and Cultural Fashions* and *Rites and Symbols of Initiation*; Joseph Guttman, *Hebrew Manuscript Painting*; Francis Huxley, *The Way of the Sacred*; Meyer Levin, *Classic Hassidic Tales*; Dorothy Norman, *The Hero*; Gershom G. Scholem, *Major Trends in Jewish Mysticism*; D. J. Tice, *The Long Road to Heaven*.

Wind-Up Sushi

with catalogues and instructions for assembly

1.

This is a litter of mice — but tin and plastic, standing on two legs, grouped like a choir, compatriot, shining: each with ceiling fluorescence riding its snout in a perfect pill-sized reflection . . . Mickey, and minions of 1940s imitation Mickeys. A glitter of mice.

One's ready to drum, if you'll wind his watch-spring gut up. One, a goggled biplane pilot, will revolve at the tip of his armature as true as a lighthouse. One somersaults. One lassoes. One tosses the cyclopean eye of a single fried egg in his skillet. Some are still: in the thirties, Japan exported over 100 bisque figurines of Mickey and his gang, some hold French horns, or banjos, or catcher's mitts, or umbrellas; these are clustered in display at the Toy Show, rough-done things, hand-painted in a very few but very declarative colors, and in the critical mass their congregating reaches, and with their soulfully-fixated blot eyes, they resemble collections of Mesopotamian votive statuettes, the kind intended to pray nonstop on behalf of their elsewhere-and-obviatingly-busy owners.

And so these toys have kept the faith—that's their appeal. While we've been busy growing up and dying down, they've been true to our childhoods, changelessly, never once diverting from their purpose, "Wind Me Up and Watch Me Play! Yoo-Hoo!"

More, later, on Mesopotamian figures. On Felix, Popeye, Flip the Frog. For now, these spokesmice say enough, say what the Whitman of their world would, if their world had a Whitman:

". . . And a toy mouse is miracle enough to stagger sextillions of toy infidels."

* * * *

The girl is five. Around her, the house; around the house, the endless dun fields of Kansas. She's the smallest living thing around that thinks. Do the cows think? She's not sure. She knows, though, that they dwarf her. They have lips the size of her hand. Their poop is wider than her whole head and, so far as she can tell, may be more valuable. Do her older brothers think and does her father? They slave for the cows—perhaps the cows out-think her family. In any case, the cows get fed with greater punctuality and verve than she does. When she's not ignored, she's in the way: her two possibilities.

What she's bigger than is Mallory, her toy friend. She can tell him how she feels. Mallory listens. Mallory's never been known to close his painted-on ears. One day a wheelbarrow of mulch bags rolls unknowingly over his back with the painted-on trousers; he snaps open like a walnut, and two spools—his heart, she guesses, and his brain—spill to the yard dirt. When she won't stop crying, the father strides over and hits her. Hits her hard, it's so annoying she'll go on like this about a goddam toy, well it's her last one then.

From corner to corner, that whole fifth year. The house around her. A mouse herself.

* * * *

I do not like that scene.

There are good guys. There are bad guys. You may think it's more complex than that, but it isn't.

My name is Jocko. I'm the Toy God.

Yeah!

Some think I'm an organ-grinder monkey. Some think I'm a hoochie-koo dancer. Whatever. I am that I am.

Just look in these here peepers deeply a second. You're getting sleepy . . . sleepy . . . Okay. So let's talk.

You think this is silly, right? Right. But I'm telling you: the dollhouse holds the toy bed, made for toy-sized sex and toy-sized praying. Of course I'm here.

You're lucky I'm talking to you at all. For us, you're like the macroverse: too vague to really exist. We have our toy dish radio telescopes beaming out messages, waiting for messages in return.

We think we hear you sometimes. Somebody very young gets through. It's like any word from the outermost vale: by the time it gets here, its source is long dead.

2.

Draw Like a True "Primitif" with LASCAUX STENCIL / One of the wittier postcards I own, it's number 216 of 300 done on textured Fabriano Artistico stock. We say that of paper: "stock." But the animals here, in umber and liver-red imitation Ice Age art, romp from before that idea. There are two bulls, there's a bison. A horse, though, is outlined in perforation. / *Cut on dotted lines. Color through stencil onto cave wall.*

I said "romp," but who knows? We're so used to them now, from having them lavishly splashed through fancy coffee-table art books, having them angled inside the prisms of cubist art: it's *their* blood-chilling panic Picasso geometricizes in *Guernica,* and in short time we've domesticated even that painting, its mangled civilian dead. GUERNICA STENCIL — it could be. "We live," Guy Davenport points out, "in a frivolously decorated world." Our small abilities for retro-understanding slam against those cave walls, and vision blacks out.

But we do understand these are no idle doodles. In, or in front of, these zoödepictions, something of the god took place.

We know that here, and at other Magdalenian sites over Europe, the sanctum caves were lightless hollows at ends of natural tunnels so low, so strenuously twisted, approach meant crawling all-fours, often through clefts that worry a modern spelunker armed electrically, but this would be by not more than a wavering flame in boar grease: "flickermittent," an art historian says. At Le Tuc d'Audoubert, a clay bull readies to mount his clay cow one-half mile into the rock—whatever that journey meant, there may be no equivalent left on this planet. Back in amnio-dark, in planet-sealant. This is serious stuff.

And by their trembling leaves of grease light, sometimes working on their backs or on the backs of others, these artists or shamans or hunter-priests—"the greatest enamelers of recorded time" is what one expert says—created beasts so exalting they wring gasps from aliens 35,000 years in the future.

Engraving was done with a flint. The fragile drawing: tufts of hair, perhaps a snipe's plume, fixed to sticks. The colors were ground from charcoal, ocher, red chalk, and manganese ore, then blown through bone tubes to the cave wall surface—it had already been prepared with a coating of oil and fat. This doesn't happen on a whim. This doesn't happen in a life that might last twenty tough years tops, unless you're driven from somewhere as deep in the mind as the caves are deep. One scholar thinks there must have been "schools" and systems of apprenticeship. At Altamira, on a rock bench there, a row of ocher crayons was found, as neat as a panpipes, each one scrupulously sharpened and in chromatic place.

From these, the bulls and their cows took shape . . . Five bulls parade the ceiling at Lascaux, the largest seventeen feet from head to tail. Or *do* they "parade?" What fear or admiration? What incredible condensing of what understanding of cosmos and self? We don't know and we'll never know. But single out even one cow in a corner, cut her from that stony herd, just one is enough, and this much is clear: it isn't play that brought men here. It's the psyche-fundament shaking.

* * * *

At the Toy Show in Topeka, Kansas, I'm looking at an Elsie the Cow just one inch high, in a vial of liquid as if she were purchased at Lourdes. It's the upper half of what once was a ballpoint pen, and can stand on its own, a quiet thing but compelling. Through the liquid, her lei of plastic daffodils floats up or down, and nimbleness (or patience) will undo and replace that adornment. She's meant to sell milk. She's intended to peddle the Borden's Dairy like any blustering sales rep. But ritually posed in this portable niche as she is, she transcends market economy. In her blue high heels and matching apron. Her classic, statuary good looks.

* * * *

Yeah!
She is one of my many consorts.

3.

Past the green-and-gold-checked fields of central Kansas, our car advances like a marker on a game board. Many fields exhibit small oil well pumps; as they rock back and forth I tell Skyler they remind me of rabbis *davening* in *shul.* Monumental toy rabbis.

So. We arrive by opening: 8:00 A.M. The Toy Show in Topeka.

* * * *

Someone's Felixes are arranged as neatly as troops for inspection. Felix in cloth, in celluloid, in printed tin, with tail and without, with rollicking googoo eyes. But somebody else's Popeyes are simply a mob. They're on the wharf, they demand higher sailor's wages. That boulder of a bicep gleams four dozen-fold. Four dozen-fold times, his pipe angles out his mouth: a babble of accent marks. It is, in a way—*toot toot*—how we best say him. Wimpy hangs around the edges, of course, in his corpulent manatee shape. And Olive Oyl. Her loony italicized anatomy is most authentically duplicated in rubber, and she's loping, or more like looping, through the Popeye throng in at least a dozen avatars.

These are choice figurines, perky of physical detail, from when Elzie Segar, Popeye's creator, was still alive.

A wind-up 1930s Popeye pummeling a red weather balloon-looking punching bag. And "Popeye the Champ" from '36: Popeye and Bluto, boxer-gloved, go at each other madly in a very credible boxing ring, until one gets kayoed against the ropes and a bell dings, ending the match. And "Popeye the Pilot." And "Popeye the Fire Fighter." When "Popeye and Olive Oyl on the Roof" gets wound (with a large tin key of the kind that used to raggedly undo sardine can lids) the sailor-man jigs frenetically, and his seated paramour (not unlike the roof-throned violinist of Chagall) is lost in the music squeezing out of her pink-pleated instrument.

The music . . . !

"Popeye the Xylophone Player." A stridently colorful pair from 1938: "Mickey the Xylophone Player" (given a major's gold shoulder fringe) and Donald Duck (not quite so jazzily uppity in costume, but whose xylophone itself is seven notes, opposed to Mickey's five). Elsewhere, Donald drums while Goofy performs a loose-limbed wobble. A singing Donald (so early, his blue-sleeved arms still end in wing-tips, not fingers). "Mickey Mouse Drummer." "Mickey Piano" (when the notes are struck, jointed figures of Mickey and Minnie, set smiling above the eight keys, artfully wiggle). "Pinky the Peddler, with Tuba." "Felix with Violin." "Benny Barfly" passes out against the honk of a bicycle horn. "Betty Boop with Flute." "Li'l Abner Dogpatch Family Band" (with Abner, the bosomy Daisy Mae, and Pappy and Mammy Yokum, all doing rinky-tink wonderfulness along the same wind-up shaft). And any number of anonymous chimps who, when they aren't mixing drinks or shaking dice or waving carnival pompoms, caper with clumsy enthusiasm in front of tin organ-grinders—their eyes seem to follow you.

(*This is only one of my many guises. Be good, bubba. I'm ever-watchful. —J*)

If there's nothing displayed in Topeka quite so rarefied as the ultra-jaunty 1931 cast-iron Mickey bank from Paris, hands on puffy hips and melon-slice smile undauntedly beamed ahead (for which, supposedly, primo Mickey collector Mel Birnkrant has turned down offers of $15,000) or, from 1929, an unauthorized meeting of Mickey and Felix the Cat, who light cigars when a lever is pulled and a flint-on-sandpaper friction device makes sparks (*baaad Mickey . . .*) — still, there's heaped treasure to tickle the eye.

Here's Flip the Frog, the bouncy brainchild of one of Disney's earliest collaborators, Ub Iwerks. It's Iwerks who drew, for instance, the first days of the original Mickey Mouse newspaper comic strip; and on the first poster ever to advertise a Mouse cartoon, Iwerks's billing is writ as large as Disney's. In 1930 he left that stable — Flip was born to compete with his elder Mouse brother — but thirty-seven Flip cartoons and six years later the Iwerks studio failed ("Flip flopped," Skyler tells me.) In 1938 Iwerks returned to Disney, where over the years he pioneered live-action/animation combo and matte technique, nabbing himself two Academy Awards.

Now, here's a Flip glazed china planter (Flip in farmer's hat is pushing a wheelbarrowish pig by its fat aft trotters) and, from '37, the "Flip the Frog Coloring Book," a lovely lively thing, with Flip astride a flying paintbrush, backdropped (spotlit really) by an immense full moon — the darkened houses below him jive like a gospel chorus, the stars are chandelier-size, and the paintbrush poking out from between his thighs is all agoo with color, spurting it mightily into this jazzy night sky to help form the book's title.

Here's the rattletrap "Amos and Andy Jalopy Taxi." "Dagwood Bumstead in Plane." Henry, that bald-headed comic strip kid who never spoke a word, is in a cart being pulled by a muskox-large swan. "Hopalong Cassidy Rocker." "Howdy Doody Clock-a-Doodle Tell-Time Clock." Little Orphan Annie jumps rope, its loop swinging craftily under her dainty tin feet. "Dick Tracy Sparkling Riot Car" and "Mortimer Snerd Crazy Car" are pacing each other in stasis. Mickey seesaw. Mickey merrily maharajah-like on an elephant's back, with Minnie aloft on its trunk. Here's Smokey the Bear in his pose of eternal arboreal vigilance. Tom Corbett, Space Cadet. "Flub-a-Dub Marionette." "Miss Mink" the hoochie-koo dancer, whose inner gears give salty shake-&-shimmy to her generous outer attributes.

(*Oh I am that I am. No form is too high or too mean for its being my vestments. Be thou ever righteous, for I abide in the low as well as the great, you bozo. —J*) Her eyes follow you everywhere.

Many of the show's visitors—it's easy to tell—are cruising for investment. Singular pieces here have appreciated 5000% since their virginal 89¢ appearance in some Depression-year Christmas stocking. Capitalists in Toyland, these bring the predator's sizing-up eye and the usurer's balance-pans hands to the avenues of delight. I do not wish to powwow with them. "There are good guys. There are bad guys," someone said to me once, though I don't know who—a voice in a dream from my childhood.

But Skyler and I have pilgrimaged here for reasons as plain as the shouting, primary reds and blues and yellows about us. "Mickey and Minnie Ballroom Dancers." "Popeye and Olive Oyl Trapeze." "Rootie Kazootie and Polka Dottie Hurdy-Gurdy Pushcart Race." "Horace Horsecollar and Clarabelle Cow Moonlight Duet Children's Piano." I don't know about those bulls of Lascaux. But *we're* "romping."

* * * *

When Skyler lay in the hospital bed, I first saw how the faces we make, making love, are also those of our worst excruciation. The med-techs hypo'd horrible subcutaneous clusters of grapes along her haunch. They wheeled her from Physical Therapy whimpering through the drug buzz. Any movement could do it, and sometimes a muscle spasmed and locked for its own mysterious actin-myosin reasons. I'd sponge her forehead or snap into bedpan service, but you know the dominant feeling was one of uselessness. Sometimes a squirming came into her face that would make the walls squirm around it.

On her second day there I brought her a stuffed dog nurse ("My real nurse is bitch enough") in Red Cross nurse's cap and cape, and holding a spoonful glob of silvery medicine (or was it a thermometer, the silver its bulb?) in one cushily padded paw. That was joined eventually by a smaller ceramic mouse nurse, plastic bottle of bubbles with bubble blower, and any number of comic books: *Nyoka the Jungle Girl, Donald Duck, Katy Keene* the glamour model protagonix with her cut-out fashion wardrobe . . .

All of this said love, of course, and all of it was accepted with that understanding. But all of it stops at the skin. Pain begins on the other side of the skin, one tissuey layer away, and pain is a possessionless and unutterably private domain.

On the other side, in the deep caves of the body, where the demon is wrestled in secret, rite goes on for only one participant, priest-and-afflicted conjoined. The walls are painted with images no one shall see, and the litanies chanted nightlong in their company shall never be spoken aloud in profane space.

I sighed and waited.

It's a tiny, in fact an invisible, sign that gets posted at the cells' gates, but a real one: NO TOYS ALLOWED.

4.

"The milo's almost in." It's that season.

She hears them talk that way, she thinks of Mallory, her dead friend. It's the most tenuous phonetic connection, yes. That's how you think when you're five. She's five—and a half. And she mourns him.

"Are the livestock in?" That's what they call the cattle. She plays word games in her head, because her own peculiar scatter-and-knot of DNA disposes her that way; and because she's learned that playing obviously—with a ball or a makeshift paper-wad doll—exposes her to ridicule; and because her attic room in the house on the land in this hard-won rural community places her in extreme isolation from friends. She plays at school a little, true. She prefers the word games there. The cattle are so important, she tells them. She says it makes her the dead stock.

In the afternoons she helps out. Dirk the younger brother's the best—he'll let her squirt him with the hose, then squirt back, YOWSH, he says, like an elephant. (She thinks: *mallophant,* and mourns her dead friend.) Then there's the foreman. He stares. She can feel his eyes, like the too-soft bellies of leeches, all up her legs and across her back. Ugh. Her mother's the worst. Well, not the worst, she just isn't there. It's frightening to see her one minute, dressed in a color like dried corn husk, the next you're staring at wallpaper that same color. The mother might touch her cheek. Faint, very faint, with no aftereffect.

By day the Kansas sky is so huge it diminishes her. It diminishes even the cows. It's pretty by day, the stupid chickens collect like foam in the shade of the henhouse, and there are those pale blue flowers, smaller than a penny, in sporadic clutches along the entire Front Road. But she walks out sometimes alone below a sky so huge, she feels herself diminishing in its grip like a sliver of soap. And at night . . . She wishes her mother could be there more, at night. (Later on, she'll learn the name of her mother's color: mallow. *Mallow-ry,* she'll think. A dead color.)

Night. Not even many stars.

"Come here."

It's the foreman. Touch it, he tells her. Take it in your mouth.

She's five. She touches it, she takes it in her mouth.

Too many stars, or not enough, and it's all in a whirl. Something's happening. What?

He carries her back to the house. His toy now.

She'll leave down the Front Road forever some day, she vows it.

For the moment: a large cardboard carton a space ship.

* * * *

Yo. Kiss mah ass.

Gotcha! Jocko here.

I enjoyed the Toy Show part, didn't you? All over, there are these temples in praise of my Being.

Look: Let's not start that *again. You're thinking I'm* not *really here? Look Jack: where there's icons there's Gods.*

There's these. These awesome statuettes, as sleek as seals, from Mesopotamia. They are so fiiine. *Their eyes as wide as does'. The quick-cut tic-tac-toe designs on their skirts. Mmm-*MMM. *The great assemblages of these reverent lads and lassies radiate such soul whomping righteousness around them you just* know *they work. They're somebody's grapnels in Heaven. From each, a little unseeable rope hangs down. They say the way ahead isn't severed.*

I mean they're real, Bosco. A catalogue says "Votive figurine, of limestone. Early Dynastic II, *ca.* 2700 B.C., *from Kish.* 5 *inches tall. This is a male, done in early 'geometric style.' The face, beard, kilt and legs are shaped as a series of inverted cones. The hands are clasped, as is typical, at the waist. The mouth is two parallel lines in the small rise of a smile. Virtually all expression rests in the eyes, which were inlaid with shell in bitumen."*

A catalogue says "This figure is crafted of chalk and painted. 6 *inches high and exceptionally well-detailed for its size, it stands in the typical arms-out-in-welcome posture. Note especially the supple curve the tail makes at a right angle to the torso."*

That's Mickey Mouse. I mean evidence, *fella. Mouse upon Mouse, in major groupings, threshold gets reached, and I hearken. Jocko hearkens, and looks down, and feels dandy. There's some forty-year-old dude right now admiring Elsie the Cow. And she tells him, "Remember: the way back isn't severed."*

Say some five-year-old gets kicked around all day. In that world she's powerless. Then she goes to her attic — wop, spanks mamadoll, oompah, bops her daddydoll up-n-down doll stairs on his head if she wants. She tells them now they're chickens if she wants. Those two worlds are so far apart they may as well be two planets.

On one of those planets I'm God.

You betcha. Now don't start again. You say it's not "really *true," the girl's making it up, in her mind, in her heart.*

Well, where did you think God dwells, huh?

Gotcha!

". . . and, in quantities, these simple figurines imply a statement larger than the sum of their parts."

5.

The placenta-red cows and mocha bulls of Lascaux are sacred business; only the High Tongue will do. But leave the caves in a timeline heading even loosely toward Topeka, and the nature of figuration grows looser.

We call it Turkey. Once it was Anatolia. Here, in 1958, James Mellaart began his exemplary excavations of Catal Huyuk, a Neolithic mud-brick town of 30 acres and 6,000 populace, situated some 50 miles northwest of the Mediterranean. This is a true town, well thought-out, and fortified. It dates to 7000 B.C., and even then was becoming an important source for distributing obsidian throughout the Near East. "Mellaart's discoveries," Davenport says, "connect history and prehistory."

David Attenborough: "A third of all the rooms found by the excavators were shrines. And in them were images of bulls." If it's only chance that puns our *cattle* with their *Catal,* then it's opportune chance. In some shrines, actual skulls are built into the walls. Bulls' heads done life-size in clay protrude from others, their long horns running along the walls almost like shallow shelving. Stylized heads of bulls, much smaller, are shaped from mud and fixed to altars: "These have been replastered and repainted as many as one hundred times, presumably during the repetition of rituals."

We also find hand-holdable models of animals, modestly, even crudely, fashioned (but no less appealing for that): toy-sized, though they might not have been toys. We don't know. We simply don't know. But children lived here as surely as priests, and just as surely had their needs. There is no formal demarcation we can draw, and from this *x* in history on, the sacred-most miniatures and the casual-most of figurines—cradle knickknacks or proto-chess pieces or recess diversions for royal heirs—play tag through time, disguise themselves as one another, grip as indistinguishably as Jacob wrestling his heavenly double, tumbling along the unlit plain.

"The clay models are sometimes interpreted as ritual objects. At Kish, however, they were found in vacant areas above the ruins of the palace, which suggests that they might be toys which were lost by children playing." —This, of two-wheeled chariot models that fit the palm (the wheels perimeter-crimped like modern bottle caps), from 2500 B.C., in Sumeria. Clay sheep, goats, dogs, onagers, and an unbroken line of cattle "are found in great number in all Near Eastern sites. The figurines are either votive models for ritual offerings . . . or toys." We simply don't know.

We do as history moves forward, of course. Context or design confirms: these two bronze boars from 500 B.C.: are toys, and from about the same time this horseman with the iron lance: is a toy, and this lion from 30 B.C.: is a toy, and its frightening wooden jaw clacks open and shut by a string run through it, and you can buy a marionette tomorrow afternoon that's basically no different. Something seems lost, though, by now. Something true seemed to be happening in the spaded-up levels of way-back, when the child's task and the priest's look so admittedly cofunctional: to take the Vast and Unexplainable Mysteries and form of them a comprehensible, manageable system.

The Pacific floor is studded with active volcanoes. The Japanese islands shake perceptibly over a thousand times a year, and Tokyo itself has been broken "an average of once a century for the past 2,000 years." In 1943, 143,000 people were killed in Tokyo and Yokohama: "We were like grains shaken in a sieve."

From this has come what Takeo Doi, a psychiatrist, calls "a consciousness of helplessness" that shapes the whole cultural mind. "Nature," Arthur Koestler says, "is too hostile and frightening to be approached 'in the raw.' To be aesthetically acceptable, it must be stylized, formalized, miniaturized." He speaks of *bonsai,* living adult trees the size of cola bottles; *bonseki,* entire landscapes to match. No wonder this is the land of fifty ivory ladies-in-waiting, with parasols, crossing an ivory bridge not six inches long. Yes, and the land of computer chip.

And toys. The smilingest shop in Austin, Texas, specializes in Japanese wind-ups: mountain climbers, trapezists, clowns, Godzillas by the crateful, an ice cream vendor, hellbent motorcyclists, paddling geese (and, if you ask, a four-star display of dogs humping) . . . My favorite's a cleaver-wielding chef absorbed in a book on gourmet cooking, and at the same time chopping (*bim bam bim* with quick precise jerks) a comically rotund poisonous blowfish. Judy once sent me a set of plastic wind-up sushi from Tokyo. I can race finger-length pieces of squid and tuna over my living room floor. They're cheap things, full of vim though, and their finger-length beds of rice look plump and moist.

So I'll buy Elsie at the Toy Show. She has quite a lineage. Daring a fudged guess here and ducking a rough spot there, I can trace it back past Hathor even, benign and bulbous cow-headed goddess of Egypt, she whose designate province is fertility (and, happily enough, fermented drink)—back to the leaping russet she-beasts of our earliest extant records of facing, of fashioning likenesses of, what can't be faced or likened: The Immanent.

If it's difficult sometimes believing the length of *her* ancestry . . . I think of that grouping of "Wind-up! Musical! Chimps!" I consider the simians.

* * * *

The pain when they forced her to stand was like a blue flame fusing bone to bone, but worse than that was what allowed it: giving up control of her body into the hands of strangers. Now that she's out of the hospital this is what, understandably so, remains the greatest ordeal: routinely they wheeled her, without her consent, from cold table to table, girl meat in a smock.

Now what's needed is the long healing at home, and one outpatient hour in the magnetic resonator: they help her into a coffin-like gizmo, then slide *that* inside the huge magnetic vault. Some people claw at its insides like premature burials. "All of my water molecules aligned. When I go swimming from now on, maybe I'll always point north."

One day while Skyler's mainly bed-bound still, I bring a set of plastic snap-together paramedics: tiny white-garbed men, with an ambulance, and a patient, and a gurney. Small white stethoscopes and white bags fit the medics. You can even set up roadblock signs for the ambulance. We use a full afternoon retelling her story in snapped-together tableaux. Many things need healing, not just bones. We direct the whole drama of it.

Skyler carries herself upstairs, one bearable hurt per jostle, then returns. She's got a child's horseshoe magnet maybe four inches tall, and she holds it upright on the table. "Look." Now we can even place the patient onto the gurney and trundle her into the magnet. Now we can laugh over that.

6.

Lindsay, my niece, is two-and-a-half. I've seen her tumble down the stairs like a rubber ball—a fall that earlier broke her grandmother's arm and likely could paralyze a seasoned Hollywood stunt man. She cried at the shock, but was laughing a minute later. Kids are like that, they have bounce. Some otherworld protection attends them. There are days when I think Lindsay could stroll unharmed through a gangland shootout, just the warm sweet smell of her being fresh from a bath would ward off bullets.

There are days I think the opposite. I watch her drawing—scribbling really, trying to get some semblance of the world clear, but botching the job. It's a tangle. She can't even do a circle and lines for the sun yet, I think, she's so small. The wind could knock her over. Certain angry words could knock her over, open furrows in her brain that won't heal for decades. Today the newspaper says an American gunboat accidentally (accidentally?) downed an Iranian passenger jet; 290 are dead "including 66 children." The evening news has shots of bloated bodies—six-foot maggot bodies—being hauled ashore. We won't let Lindsay watch.

She wakes scared in the night.

"Could Mommy die?"

"That's silly, Lindsay," I tell her. "Your Mommy's not going to die."

"Could you?"

"Not tonight. Go to sleep."

We're all so small. It's what the wind knows, biding its time, as it toys with us on a mild spring day.

* * * *

Pegleg Pete was Evil Incarnate. Mickey Mouse's nemesis for sixty years now, Pegleg Pete was there from the beginning, leering, robbing coaches, spitting enormous swashes of tobacco juice into the ozone, plotting bank heists, nabbing Minnie whenever he could (in those long-ago days when that would have placed her "in his clutches"), swearing up the kind of exclamationpoint-lightningbolt-asterisk blasphemy-storm that soiled many a comic book's otherwise wholesome air, and—in between achievements, just to keep his nefarious conduits lubricated—rubbing his hands together in unctuous anticipation of bullying yet to come. He'd even cheat to win a fistfight.

He was grossly overweight, a bulldog-looking cat thing packed near bursting with fat and muscle in unholy combination, and of course . . . *tap* . . . *tap* . . . there was that nightmarish wooden peg in support of that nightmarish bulk. The idea of being without a body part, of so basic a malformation, was horror even beyond the list of his criminal infamies. And he was always *there*. When Mickey traveled out West, it was Pegleg Pete rustling cattle. When Mickey joined the Foreign Legion — stirring the tribesmen up, embroiling whole nations in desert war: yep, Pegleg Pete.

As first drawn for the May 5, 1930 *Mickey Mouse* comic strip by master Mouse artist Floyd Gottfredson, that peg is grotesquely in high relief against shadow, as the villain leaps on Mickey, declaring, "Lemme at him! He may be the apple of Minnie's eye — but he'll soon be applesauce!" On October 21, 1942, appeared the famous strip in which the hooligan seems to be stomping about on two normal legs. "What about the old wooden kicker?" asks Mickey. The answer (coming in the accents of his disguise as a French northwoodsman): "Ah . . . I hav' replace heem with new model store leg! Pierre, she's now streamline lak' modern design, eh?" By 1950s comic books, he was Pete; Pete purely. The stinking cigar was gone too. Oh, he still relished robbing the nearest bank, but lost to the sanitized fifties was his joy in kicking a wizened bank guard, just for the hell of it, on his way out. He probably had insecurity problems like anyone, and deserved a fair hearing.

By now, I may as well be talking about the hospital orderlies. Their laxness or their crudeness was a torment for Skyler — prodding where they shouldn't, never around when they should. But you know they were just sad underpaid bastards, schleps in the hierarchy, doing their jobs.

A voice, insisting: "There are good guys. There are bad guys." But another voice says being grown-up is knowing how everyone's marbled by both, until even the definitions blur and we all walk around in a tumult of ethical relativism. I *know* that I'm kind (six plastic paramedics in white jackets form a chorus line behind me, crooning my praises) but every Iranian knows I'm a citizen of the nation they call "The Great Satan." I'm not so fond of them. Who *does* live in our mirrors?

So there's something compelling, touchingly compelling, in this 1930's pop-up book: Mickey and Pegleg duking it out ("Take that, you!") on a cliff's edge. Popeye and Bluto (who was Pegleg's suit size) tussling on behalf of, respectively, Ultimate Justice and Ultimate Greed. Dick Tracy. Buck Rogers. Good guys. The most popular of all adorned the hospital wall, in his standard figurine pose: on a cross. He's been given a Bad Guy of Bad Guys, to match.

In a Jewish legend the world is saved from destruction each day by the *lahmed vov,* the "thirty-six hidden saints," is saved because they *exist,* they don't do anything out of the way. That's the point: they don't even know who they are. One might be a king and one a scholar of holy writ, but one might just as easily be collecting the village's sheep shit to dry for fuel. A cobbler, a wet nurse, the one over there dealing cards all night in a corner — who knows? It's their hearts. They simply need to be themselves, and God holds back His punishing hand.

There are no figurines, how could there be? They say, from who- and wherever they are, that this is the most grown-up of all. Flash Gordon preens with his ray guns drawn and his Galaxy Rangers badge agleam in silver, and next to him Hojo the Hobo is contemplating infinity. We must cherish them all, with no model to go by, the Peddler, the Barfly, cherish them all.

7.

My father was in his twenties in the Depression. *His* father went blind — glaucoma clouded the jellies. Everything was scrimped: left-over rinds of bread for stuffing, candle drippings for weeks to become new candles. My father hauled ass over twelve-hour days inside the vat rooms where the paints got mixed, and even after lead poisoning burned his veins he kept on dollying the tubs from dock to flat bed until one afternoon, with the heat inside the mixing shed in the hundreds, he dropped. They were poor, the gauzes they'd press to his arms were the same ones used that morning on his father's eyes. A time like this will sand shapes into the grain of a whole generation. No one who comes to it later will understand. Know, maybe — but not understand.

His health recovered; the finances, barely; his worldview, never: something called "waste" was the primary sin. Eating a home-cooked meal was the primary good, and cleaning one's plate was its single greatest devotional.

With that said, it's surprising how surely a profligate he was with the family's meager funds, in populating my toy chest. I'd hardly say I was "spoiled," by any current upscale standard. "Opulent" wouldn't be true. And yet Bluey the Pig, Geronimo Monkey, Jasper the Giraffe, a clown, two overheaping handfuls of plastic soldiers, that prankster Sammy the Squirrel . . . their society never failed in welcoming me, and though Bluey was chipped so a raw cedilla of plaster showed through one cerulean ear, though Sammy's paint had been sweated away by my grip till his red vest looked like measles, this was no more than if Jimmy Katzamanis from down the block appeared at my door with crutches — as best as we could, we played together.

Thirty years later (let's say I was ten) I can easily picture Geronimo, his monkey tail enspiraled over his head like some quotation mark forever beginning to cite him . . . In the dark of the chest, while I slept. They kept vigil. They had adventures. Buddies.

Much of my father's tolerance was, I think now, simple unmuddied goodheartedness; and a lower-middle-class vow his generation made for its children to know the gratuities *it* couldn't. From Merwin's versions of Antonio Porchia's aphorisms: "A child shows his toy, a man hides his." My sister and I may have been my father's implicit giving in to this wisdom.

Let's say I was ten — my sister swears she was five. All week we'd practiced wheedling the chance to garner ourselves some Charms: cheap plastic toylets in clear plastic bubbles you'd get for five cents from a vending machine. I can't say *why* we wanted them, diffidently-created bland spaceman or kittycat shapes that, even then, we knew were essentially soulless.

But that didn't temper our Most Ferocious and Unctuous Imploring. It wasn't the five cents only — the store was on the wrong side of Division Street, where manic cars splattered children for kicks, and pederasts were known by my parents to gather each night in conventioneer number. An adult had to accompany us. Charms, we wailed, Charms.

He thought they were a candy. Although candy drifted through teeth with the sure destructive power of sand through ancient ruins, it partook—if dimly—of the sacred category "food." And so on a weekend night, when rest was his due, by our persistence and his mistaken notion, we set off three of us hand-in-hand for Dishkin's Variety Store.

I won't belabor the telling any further. The point is, halfway there it struck him through some conversational slip of ours that these Charms weren't edibles. Disappointment showed in his face—it hit me like a shovel. I could see he felt betrayed, felt his good will was misapplied, and then in under a second I saw him understand how his initial willingness needed nonetheless to be carried out. His face absorbed the disappointment—it was like watching that same shovel thrown back into a pool, the surface calming above it.

So we bought those Charms on the frantic side of Division Street. I wanted to squeeze mine into my palm until I bled—what I'd witnessed of the graciousness of being a father was too hard to bear.

Now thirty years dwindles that anecdote. Too much love is in the way, and too much piddlyshit. Three decades of newspaper headlines intervene, and the divorce papers. Some of what's happened—it's not worth wiping your ass with. Other moments, maybe even so small as a wooden coffee stirrer someone's gentleness gives dignity to in a diner off I-35—well, it pulls the breath from you like a magician's scarf. And then one day you're visiting your mother's, shuffling through his . . . what do they call it? . . . his effects. And what are you doing now, a shovel in your grip, working down to the bedrock?

I don't remember those plastic trifles we'd schemed a full week of our lives for.

I remember that split-second look on his face.

* * * *

Quoting from an essay by psychologist Ellen Winner: "As early as age two children's spontaneous scribbles become explicitly pictorial. They often begin with scribbles but then, noticing they have a recognizable shape, they label and further elaborate it. One three-and-a-half-year-old studied his scribble and called it 'a pelican kissing a seal.' Another child made seemingly unreadable marks, looked at his picture, and said with confidence, 'Chicken pie and noodies!' "

"What do you have here, Lindsay?" my sister asks.

It's a mild spring day. The crayons are scattered over the grass like toy soldiers in uniform: red army, yellow, green. Lindsay holds up her page. *Nonrepresentational* isn't the word. Psychedelic spaghetti, maybe. I roll my eyes.

"A moo cow."

It is?

breathing concentration breathing. "See this is the moo part . . ." *breathing concentration breathing.* ". . . and this is the cow part."

It is. Now I can see it, truly, now that its critical exegesis has been delivered with such élan.

* * * *

. . . That's the vignette I have in my mind as the dealer at Table 3 scrupulously wraps Elsie. (He throws in an Elsie comic book, "Elsie and Elmer Vacation Fun.") She's leaving with me, from her sisterhood of Elsie milk mugs, flowerpots, pinback buttons, toothbrush holders, rubber stamp sets, pencil cases, "sip-&-see straws," rings and pendants, lunchboxes, serving trays, paper dolls with cut-out changes-of-bovine-wardrobe, sand pails, rulers, jigsaw puzzles, Elsie in glass and in ceramic, Elsie excelsior, ample and wise.

I will leave with her on my dashboard.

This cow will drive this man home.

* * * *

Yeah! Yowza. Yessir. Jocko here. I liked that part about the "moo cow." Cute. And Gods enjoy stories about creation on lesser levels. And finding-patterns-after-the-fact-in-what-seemed-chaos shtick. It gets a God, a Toy God even, right in the ol' nut-meat. Say, that reminds me: you were promised "instructions for assembly." It's up in the title, go check. So I'm going to . . . oh, wait. Excuse me, somebody's coming.

(KA-ZHOOM! *A cardboard spaceship lands.)*

Well. Welcome, little girl, to the planet Planet. You can play here all you'd like until you fall asleep. I won't let them hurt you. I'll give you some toys in a moment, you can put them together. Just let me talk to this grown-up first.

Where was I, Bunko? . . . oh yeah, assembly. I have to hurry, I've got this little girl. She needs special attention. Put the Lindsay parts together. Put the Skyler parts together. Take the cave parts and the Elsie parts and snap them together on either side of the sushi. Then the Mickey and Felix and Popeye and Flip parts — those parts make a border for the rest. If you listened, the whole shmear's gonna balance like a mobile. Gonna jangle, gonna twirl in the morning light.

I'd like to chat with you some other time, Herman. But right now, you know, the little girl.

You're going to forget me now. When you wake, you'll be on the road back home from Topeka. That's the way it works.

Go put it together. Don't worry, Doc. A five-year-old can do it.

(Snap)

* * * *

On the way home, Skyler browses a bag and discovers the comic book perk. She reads it assiduously as lowering sunlight glows in molten bars through the car.

Hawk silhouettes. Some scraggly stands of Russian olive. Mainly, corn and grazing land. While Elsie and Elmer frolic at the beach or in crevasses of the Matterhorn, the cows of Kansas heavily move their heavy lips over late spring tufts. They look as if they're confiding something.

Skyler: "When I was a child I wasn't allowed to read comic books. Never. They thought the Bible should have been enough. I didn't really have many toys. I never heard of Little Lulu." There was a Little Lulu bank at the Toy Show, faithful to the carat nose and long ringleted hair of the stories I grew up with.

It makes me crazy to knock at my father's stone, and rouse him from worms, from seraphs, and gather the bones like the parts of a very old and clumsy communication system, fitting them together, mortar, pestle, maracas and bannister bones, and old ledges of schoolroom chalks, until I can put my lips, at last, to the mouthpiece and whisper a message — *thank you* — so long delayed in the saying, the language has changed.

* * * *

We pass a highway exit sign for CATTLE PENS, and Skyler lifts my ballpoint Elsie into the light — a silent pun.

"But I'm going to have toys now," she says.

Yes. For all the right reasons that brush against love, she's going to have toys now.

Mel Birnkrant, one of the country's three or four elite Mickey Mouse collectors, began his exemplary mouseum of delights when he found a cast-iron Mickey bank in a Paris flea market — I've described it briefly, in section three. "It seemed to me incredible as sculpture, but the Mickey aspect gave me pause. I had given away all my Mickey things from childhood. But then I thought: 'I like this kids' stuff. Maybe growing up is *admitting* you like it.'"

The oil pumps nod in agreement.

* * * *

Listen: this is what I believe. A small black plastic rabbi resides at the center of Earth, at the pit of its iron core. One of the inexpensive kind. A wind-up rabbi, rocking back and forth, and back and forth . . . So long as he *davens,* the planet spins. So long as someone believes in him, he *davens.*

Ellen's

I.

Turning and turning in the guiding wire.

* * * *

The phone rings.

Collect, long distance. "Albert it's Ellen I'm in Kalamazoo and singing in the park"

"Kalamazoo?"

"by the fountain. I'm singing by the fountain in the park."

So it's An Ellen Call.

"And the people like it but I'm wondering should I sing for free and sleep in the park by the fountain"

If voices have eyes, these two are round as the moons in a child's drawing.

"or charge for my singing and sleep in a hotel."

"Does your sister know where you're at?"

"She doesn't like my singing oh Albert"

"Ellen?"

"Let's rent a xerox machine and have a party and xerox our bodies and make a frieze of all of our friends on the wall."

"When you get back. Ellen, what's your sister's number?"

* * * *

Ellen is in her thirties. It's 1969, she's been my friend three years but I've never seen her depressed. I've never seen those moons' dark sides.

* * * *

"Albert it's Ellen I was wondering"

"Hey, Ellen, hi."

"if you want to build a raft this summer and float down the Mississippi like Huck and Nigger Jim I know it sounds crazy"

"It sounds a little crazy."

"but I've got the details worked out how to construct it and charts of the currents and navigation laws so don't worry."

Some nights, plenty moonshine.

"No, I'm not worried."

"We could sing songs on the raft."

* * * *

All of this is serious on Ellen's part, and not without a full comprehension of how it sounds to those of us not touched by the light of her mania: wondrous, stuff-o'-dreams, disaster-bound, retardate. In fact Ellen is the most intelligent friend I have — her IQ an apogee.

My lesbian divorcée single-mother friend Ellen the poet.

* * * *

"It's . . . Ellen."

Collect (to Chicago) long distance (from Bakersfield, California). I'm living at home. My father extends the phone as if it were powered by fecal matter. His eyes roll up to God, the sign of a kind of cynicism they share.

"Hi, Ellen. What's up."

"Well I'm okay really"

I won't say much until my father leaves, and the stalling is costing him money. His pupils return like a one-arm-bandit's indicating of jackpot. He leaves.

"but I thought Sammy might like to visit his father who lives in California so one day we got in the car with Mr Bones the dog and just left and *that* was okay"

"Where's Sammy now?"

"but we lost Mr Bones around Arizona because we ran out of food and he was hungry and *that* was okay because we made California"

"Look, where are you calling from?"

"and when Sammy ran from the motel room I ran out to get him back of course though I was mostly naked not completely but mostly I had to run out fast"

"Uh huh."

"so when the cop stopped me I hit him."

"Oh, Ellen."

"That wasn't so okay."

Sammy's in the custody of the state of California. Ellen's to remain there, for study. Sammy might be allowed to come back home, to his grandparents . . . will I contact them?

I'll contact them.

I'll make any number of calls in the next few weeks, to any number of friends, all of whom love Ellen.

The cord of the phone, its dozens of spirals.

"Anyway, how are they treating you?"

The long, the very long, distance.

"Okay. They won't let me sing after lights-out though."

2.

"Swervings into fantasy"—a phrase from Kenneth Clark, on the notebooks of Leonardo da Vinci.

He says: "Leonardo was fond of drawing artesian screws and other spiral devices. On a sheet of doodles in the *Codice Atlantico* he had drawn such a spiral for its own sake, and he has endowed it with a kind of monstrous life, so that it changes, like Aaron's rod, into a serpent."

Years later, I can see that spiral as perfectly emblematic of my friend Ellen Dapple's manic (and, as I'd discover, depressive) reactions. Not that I necessarily think Leonardo shared in her biochemical distress; the records-taking of Ellen's brain, in its secret convolute script, was urgent—and I can't speak for how casual may have been the perceptions of what Clark calls "this interweaving of fact and fantasy in Leonardo's mind."

I only know I think of the notebooks, done in his backwards hand, demanding a mirror: and after ten years Ellen is clear again in my revery: dear, and diligent, and chronicling my world truly in her head: though in her own special coded reversals.

This essay-of-sorts will turn to Ellen again, a bit later, will . . . well, spiral back. For the spiral's supremacist, though, we need to look to Daedalus: Athenian, mage of mazes, he whose name means "the cunning maker." Michael Ayrton has him say: "I am a thickset man, inclined to run to fat. My legs are weak and I am a little lame in one of them." Gide, in what seems contradiction: "He was very tall, and perfectly erect." —No matter. Here he is really: bunch-browed, bent to the task, his whole face: white light focused through thought-like-a-lens, burning its way to a problem.

Which has been set him, the legend goes, by King Cocalus of Sicily: ". . . a spiral shell, offering a large reward to anyone who could pass a linen thread through it." No sweat. This is the man who devised "the three-legged tables, with golden wheels, which would run by themselves to their owner's side when he commanded." Orderly in his catalogues are weapons-of-war the size of modern-day battleships, with feasible catapult mechanisms and moat-digging motorized jaws requiring sometimes tens of dozens of grunting winch-turners, sometimes just a kettle of steam; and ladies' intimate devices the size of peas, oh the size of silver peas in a satin-and-lacquer case.

Today, on a Sicily beach, it's easy. The olive trees bounce sun like thousands of drab-uniformed schoolchildren. A bird cuts a leisurely corkscrew, down, and down. He yawns: a cave of garlic, lemon-brushed squid, a little only, ruby wine. "Drilling the shell at the top, Daedalus tied a strand of gossamer to the leg of an ant, which he induced up through the whorls by smearing honey around the drilled hole. Then he joined the linen thread to the end of the gossamer and drew it through."

You see him? That man, there . . . "On the beach?" Yes, licking his fingers.

* * * *

It is told how Minos, contending against his brothers for the throne, would pray, at the day's three Holy Junctures, that the god Poseidon send up a bull from the sea, as sign of Minos's ascendancy, "and he had sealed the prayer with a vow to sacrifice the animal immediately, as an offering and symbol of service." For many days: the brass bowls on the altars, ropes of incense-smoke. And then the prayer was answered. And Minos was king of the island-empire Crete.

The bull was pure white — as if fashioned of sea-foam itself. The light rode its flanks like epaulets. Minos beheld it — something about the lustrous horns, its bellycurve up to the cock, the cock like a counting-house chute, its almost-goosedown snout . . . He added the beast to his herd, and on Poseidon's altar substituted a gray-white bull of his own, a good one though, a good one.

And so it's tempting to say: Poseidon's wrath inspired the lust of Pasiphaë, wife of Minos. Who knows? You draw the spiral-line of the inner ear, the cochlea, snailshape whorl on whorl, and finally who's to say on which side falls the voice of the gods, on which the voice of a man's own congenital counselors.

Or a woman's. In any case, one day Pasiphaë beheld the bull . . .

And brought her need to Daedalus. Which was, in all, a simple need and they say the contrivance was simple.

It's simple today. The gland-man straps them by snout to the ceiling pulleys, cranks them from feedpen to breeding-rack. The prepuce is scrubbed. Sometimes the attendant's hand's insinuated up the rectal pudge, and massages away. The slit in the dummy-cow's steel rump is scented. That's the important thing.

And they / *hey diddle-diddle* / spasm, once, into water-warmed rubber. They're married to seventeen inches of engineered vinyl and the ring in the nose gleams.

Talk about spirals: 15,000 coiled feet of tubing in the testicles of a bull.

Pasiphaë knelt, all fours, the understructure was ventilated with ribbing and yet the cowhide over it all kept most of the heat in. Daedalus measured well: though inches of unlit air surrounded her face, her gooseflesh breasts, her tensed arms up to the shoulders: here, where the worlds would meet and it counted, her rump was flush with the cowskin. And its slit was scented. That was the simple, that was the important, thing.

The offspring was a monster. Birthed in pain, and soon thereafter a painful sight, the Minotaur required hiding. This is the simple story of how a complex thing is done. And it was done. The sun shone full upon it. Daedalus smiled. I think at a sense of completion, something having clicked with the final brick into place. And no sun shone inside it, at all. The smile was short, a hyphen, it connected him to the rest of the day, a workday like all days and so he turned from the world of kings to the world of cogs and counters.

The Labyrinth "commemorates him as the ancestor of all the celebrated architects of the Western world."

And the father, of course, of Icarus.

There were adventures: pourings of blood, semen dried to a knee's-crook, something gold . . . The world of kings, like cogs, will turn. It tells the time. It tells you when the time is up. For this in one version, for that in another, Daedalus and Icarus, insubordinate, arm-linked, rag-shod, were imprisoned in the Labyrinth.

You know about the wax-fashioned wings. Ellen's sister once did a series of prints, *Icarus Descending*. His face, like that on a coin, starts shining; and then the quick use rubs it blurred. Finally he's sunken treasure; the death gives us Breughel's painting, Auden's poem. Riding a low safe flight line, Daedalus landed in Sicily, stumbled along the beach, and lay his first night with his arms still strapped to the flap-hinges and his cheek in a puddle of salt. He'll wake grieving. He'll learn to carry the grief. That salt will flavor the rest of his days, though not to bitterness. In Ayrton's novel, he's left as an old man calmly, in a humming garden, listing by way of summation the symbols of one human life spent working out mazes. Here's how I leave him: just taken off, the air a palpable crutch-rest under each arm, his beeswax holding, all the sky become his home, and he's that jointed be-feathered scallop-wing figure we picture dangling, working the quills, across the cream-color heavens that's a page from the note-books of Leonardo.

* * * *

Clark: "The most curious man in history." He sets aside his sepia schema of man-in-flight, and focuses now on — anything. "Why does one find sea-shells in the mountains? How do they build locks in Flanders? How does a bird fly? What accounts for cracks in walls? What is the origin of wind and clouds? How does one stream of water deflect another? Find out; write it down; if you can see it, draw it." Spirals: maelstroms, whirlpools, screw threads thrust in seasoned wood, and most especially the slippery loops of the human body.

"Leonardo discovered a centenarian in a hospital in Florence, and waited gleefully for his demise so that he could examine his veins. Every question demanded dissection and every dissection was drawn with marvelous precision."

Here: the fetus wrapped in its natal coils, tight as a watchspr-ing readying Time. Leonardo, bent with pen, to the shadowed whorls of the pinna, to the kidney coils, the ampersands lining the lung.

In *Rites and Symbols of Initiation,* Eliade considers the shape, and our necessary confronting of it: "the labyrinth is presented as a 'dangerous passage' into the bowels of Mother Earth, a passage in which the soul runs the risk of being devoured" before it exits — if it does — to a next life.

So. Here's Leonardo, over a bowel.

Here's Leonardo studying the thirty coiled feet of a human gut — which is, itself, a kind of studying: funneling ever finer, bringing it all to a distilled point, deciding what to reject, what to keep to go on with.

Dissection was new. It's worth repeating what we know of the times: no antiseptics, no refrigeration — not running water, even. The stink was almost visible, mucused-over and splotched. He did some thirty bodies. Sometimes he used small blades. He had to know. If needed, his nails.

3.

The very form, if it's to be perceived as a form at all, requires our focus — takes our vision around and, in going around, exacts it. Not, then, that the spiral *inspires* meditation; to see the spiral *is* to meditate. And so the mandala.

This: "In 1902 Fakir Agastiya of Bengal, India, raised one arm straight above his head." In three months the circulation cut off completely. A bird built its nest in his palm. He died in 1912, the arm still raised, and was duly buried that way.

With this concentration, imperturbable, whole, the successful initiate becomes — not looks at: *becomes* — what Giuseppe Tucci calls "an immense mobile mandala." The two-dimensional pattern we know from the printed page radiates from the mystic in blazing foliate-bangled tentacular convolutions: "Shining round about, the divine matrices of things come forth from the center of his own heart, pervade space, and then re-absorb themselves in him." — He novas.

Is he culturally preconditioned to see the expected shape? "C. G. Jung discovered such forms emerging from the psyches of his European patients, the majority of whom knew nothing about mandalas. The production of these mandalas came to his attention 'long before I knew their meaning or their connection with the strange practices of the East.'"

— It's the East. An adept's vision is hovering over a circle of many involuting galactic pathways.

Or: a bee, above a full rose.

A lover's tongue at the cunt-lips.

Many bees, and many roses — it's a topiary, the Minotaur done at its center out of alabaster. The visitor's eyes: around, around.

A man drops to his knees. And then his entire body, under desert noon, assumes the tremulous supplication of a kneel. His name is Ezekiel. The Bible says he saw wheels of eyes, saw chariots, flaming, on wheels of eyes. Well of course he did.

He'd been concentrating.

* * * *

Ellen practiced yoga. Ellen went to The Meditation Center. She had a mantra, and sang it for me. It made the phone's transistorized circuits, a moment only, mandalas in mandalas in mandalas; then the disconnecting click, and the long empty hum.

* * * *

Jung ends one of his seminal works: "As the historic parallels show, the symbolism of the mandala is not just a unique curiosity; we can well say that it is a regular occurrence." Okay. A history of doodles, shard on rock, Bic pen to butcherpaper: thousand-foot serpentine earthworks, Navajo sand-paintings, tree rings in ink, green eddies in chalk: a species' history. For Jung, it has many possible guises, and some I'll list later.

For now, though, this. The work that I've just quoted from is *Individual Dream Symbolism in Relation to Alchemy*. One patient's dream in analysis: "At all events the spiral emphasizes the center and hence the uterus, which is a synonym frequently employed for the alchemical vessel, just as it is one of the basic meanings of the Eastern mandala."

Charlatans there were, aplenty, dropping dung in a cheap alembic, muttering Latinate mumbo-jumbo, stirring with *this ancyent Philosophers Wand,* then dribbling the gook out to reveal *a Nuggett of Gold New-Mayd,* and thence cast as a florin, and wasn't the wonder-maker toasted well and wrapped warm about by the court ladies, wasn't he subsidized with guilders up past the flaps of his ermine cap! (The gold was hidden in the wand, and loosened by stirring.)

There were, too, the other kind—fewer, less florid. *Laboratory* comes from the alchemist's workshop: *labor,* and *oratorium* (place devoted to prayer). For these, "moral virtues were required," their real object was "the perfection or at least the improvement of man" — the maze of alchemical tubing: emblematic of inner refining. The monster. Trying to face it.

* * * *

It's Texas. The West. A man, one morning, sees his face in the bathroom sink: shimmer, break, collect again, then spiral down the drain.

He walks out, thinking his friends, their baggage of griefs. A woman he loves, but her face shimmered, broke, and was never repieced. Then it's night. The leaves whirled in the yard. Back home, in bed, there isn't any mandala, just the darkness. Just the darkness, nothing more.

Unless it's the swirl in his navel.

Unless it's his own identity-gyre.

He's trying to face it all, now. He's making this sentence, a word at a time: the spool of typewriter ribbon: unwinding.

4.

Ellen is huge. Her movements, in their affinities, are birdlike: shy and dainty. Translated up through amazonian compilings of bone and muscle, they seem to be the movements of bulldozers, pile drivers, airport security systems. You have to look hard to see the nest inside the steel girders.

But it's there, and the bird coos. Ellen collects the folk songs from her Ohio chalk quarry birthland. She tapes herself to better learn its rhythms — when to hold, and when to let go of, authenticity. Based on this, she's writing a folk opera using the plot of *Deirdre*. And she's a poet. Much of her work is concerned with an Amazon figure, vital, proud and ungainly. Ellen's eyes and lips, such eloquent sensitized apparatus, are lost in a head too vast — as if a delicate Japanese flower were glazed as the central device of a heavy Amish family-sized serving platter.

Sammy was accidental, at something like sixteen. Soon he was Ellen's alone, and by his prodigious IQ and equivalent shoe size, you can tell. He's twelve. He sits in a circle of beers and drinks his chocolate milk and argues aesthetics. He's tall but short of friends. He's invented conceptual baseball, solitaire, by throwing his key ring. The number of keys facing out, or in, or clustered according to certain rules, the variables of configuration: all this dictates runs about the bases. Ellen's always back by his bedtime. One day they find Mr Bones, this wasted dog with cat's-cradle hips, and bring him home. They clean up the crap together.

At parties, Ellen's warmth is so intense it solders. There we are, in a circle, dancing, and she's the heat in our hands. She's crowned with a dandelion wreath. She tells the story of when she was young and got the peanut stuck in her nose. She laughs so hard she pees. Later, drunker yet, her urine-soaked boots drying off by the fire, she talks about her theory of circularity in poetic form and alternately sucks on the stems of her dandelions.

Her love life, though, is bleak. For a time she experiments with a group of lesbian poets. A member dances in pasties and a ruby-sequin G-string. When a lover knocks unexpectedly at the back door one midnight, dressed in a forest-green hunting jacket, riding breeches, black leather boots, with a leather crop and a huge fake handlebar moustache, Ellen drops out of the group — these scenes aren't good for Sammy. Later, taking a class, she meets Jerry O'Geary. That really is his name. He writes poems, he carries a key ring more populous than Sammy's, his one piece of furniture is a refrigerator — that's all I remember. Ellen writes me a letter: she's just bought a sheer black nightie. The whole page sings and blushes.

She holds a clerical job in the Art Department. Part time, she's completing her Master's Report — something about the prose of Joyce as a geometric figure. Ellen explains, she's concentrating on how the language itself is labyrinth-like — circuitous, many-appendaged, spiraling out and in — while listing all the references to mazes in the text itself. She tells me she gets lost in her work.

The things she tells me! We're sitting on Josh's lawn, near done with a bottle of Portuguese white. He's had a lamb roast, everyone's mouth is greased like a clown's. The carcass is still on the spit and a few of the more determined celebrants still do Neolithic dance steps around it. I'm trying hard not to crack my cracked plastic cup even more. But it's the only thing to fidget with. The stars have come out, like confidantes saying it's okay now, and Ellen's explaining her Joyce visions.

When she's troubled lately, he comes with advice. Not bodily, no gray shape from beyond the grave, nothing hokey like that. But say she's been throwing a problem around, from one cerebral hemisphere to another, back and forth. And at the critical moment, Joyce Brothers Movers rounds the corner — its timely van. A random rippling of newspaper pages opens to Joyce Shoes Annual Sale. It happens this way, over and over, she tells me quiet and matter-of-fact, whenever she's troubled she has this vizier.

Sammy's growing truculent. Why not? He's pushing thirteen, and it's pushing back. She tells me, though not in these words, that Jerry O'Geary is losing interest. They still see each other, etc, but he's seeing other women too, etc. You know. We all march against the war. But Ellen marches harder. She sits down in a suburb jail and won't stand up. She studies the papers, you have to *know* your enemy. Black limousines follow her home. She checks the couch for hidden microphones. It's rose-pattern, you could hide anything in it. She doesn't want to hit Sammy.

One morning Jerry O'Geary calls, I think from a pay phone. Ellen's just committed herself to a state-run mental facility. She's asked for me. Would I visit?

I'll visit.

* * * *

It's ten years later, I live in Texas now. And sometimes I still walk out at night, as I did in the razor-sharp snows of Chicago, and pray for my friends — or myself, in some kinds of darkness it's hard to distinguish sure outlines.

Not an orthodox prayer. A kind of well-wishing made in the small, the personal, mandalas of the skull's two semi-circular canals — where we keep our balance.

5.

Androgeus, a fully human son of Minos, was slain by a score of Athenian rowdies. Minos, by then a Mediterranean power, demanded retribution: seven young Athenian men and seven Athenian maidens, every nine years, would be shipped to Crete as tribute, and there given over to the hungers of the Minotaur. In the third such group—it's eighteen years since Daedalus limned the final perfect block in place—is the son of Aegeus the king of Athens: Theseus.

According to one source: "He slew the Minotaur with his fists." Another: "Theseus was able to despatch him, driving the sword through his body and then cutting off his head." —It's been a long while, the panhellenic sun dazzles the edges of details.

This we know for sure: Ariadne waited, just a step inside the mossed-over mouth. Her breasts were bare, and lightly perspired, and cold enough today to be projection of the rock. Her gauzy skirt: a ground fog. Only one thing moved: the clew of linen thread. It started waist-high and as wide as a pantry door. But now it fit in her hands like an injured bird, unraveling.

—Where we get the meaning usually given its other spelling, "clue." And Theseus, figuring it out—by the yard, by the great taut length of attachment, spiral twist and spiral backtwist, literal: figuring / it / out.

There are thousands of versions of the battle, it's difficult *not* to make it horrific and adventuresome. I refer you to those available in English; you can follow every acrid desperate slash in the torch-splashed darkness. What I'm interested in is the memoir found on a fire-blackened parchment scrap, in Theseus's effects, and bearing a smudged Athenian seal. It starts mid-sentence "not as you would believe, and not as I would have believed had I not seen it. The very step-in and traversing of the ill-lit fenestration-ways, was test of mettle—and truly, as I have recounted, I doubted; my muscles doubted, my spit; and I was afraid. Long after, the tunnels unwound, to face the monster was further terror; he was of fierce aspect, and whether it was courage or simple enervation that held me, today I could not say. And then the fight, and now you understand why I write this holding my nib in a grip more scar than flesh. But then the Minotaur died and the worst came.

"On the floor of the pit of the central-most cavern he curled. He said once the name of the bull and the name of his mother — the voice was a burble of blood — and then his spirit left. I could study him now, in the calm. His head was slightly turned and the lips gone softly away from their living snarl. It was anybody's face — I had seen my own, in many a standing pool, on many a day, twist beastly more than this. His knees and hands were drawn into his belly. Having spoken what was unspeakable of his coming to be, he came to pass, and in death his likeness to me — or so it seemed then, after flurry — made me stroke him once with either hand, a tremble, as if to say one shook in revulsion; and one with tenderness.

"I ran back to Ariadne . . ." (*— in rough translation*)

Plucking the thread back up, to the light at the mouth. Their kiss is famous. She threw the last bit left of the thread to the breeze.

There's a legend: the thread raveled up and flew off. The shape of a healed bird.

* * * *

A man walks Texas, thinks of friends: Carolyn, Micheline, Lune: the last so high once on a manic jag, she masturbated past pain to blanking out. They're all, now, stabilized on lithium pills. The stellar bursts, the vast black spaces: in balance. This makes a working night sky.

And what of the woman, her name I can't use, my ex-fiancée whose griefs were not — and so whose curing couldn't be — chemical. Over a year since I've seen her. Where can she look to. Sometimes I walk all night. Her shrink recommended hypnosis. There are myths in the nervous system.

— The stories, the figures up there that the stars figure out.

The bulls. The spiral nebulae.

6.

Theseus conducts his carnage and coronations in myth. For Philipson: "Leonardo is infinitely more significant as a myth than as a man." And de Santillana: "Leonardo is, precisely, an irreducibly mythic personality."

(But I want to conjure him callus-footed, worrying a peach pit in his cheeks, and walking the tideline: grumbling, distracted, a funny old cluck, just before dawn and he's the only stick out stirring this soupy air. And thinking: eddies; thinking: whorls. "Leonardo was obsessed by the study of water." "A sheet at Windsor shows water taking the form of both hair and flowers, racing along in twisted strands, and pouring from a sluice so that it makes dozens of little whirlpools." The shape of it. Meditating.)

"Leonardo was an Oriental. His thoughts on art and nature would ravish Indian, Chinese, or Japanese readers." I can't say if that means a mandala-pattern was one of his psyche's natural modes of expression. But Heinrich Wölfflin, describing the "dream-like . . . brown, green-blue and blue-green" background of the *Mona Lisa,* chooses to start: "fantastic, jagged labyrinths of mountains."

Then: "They are of a different order of reality from the figure (of Mona Lisa herself)." The idea of bifurcation runs through studies of Leonardo, unavoidably.

Often it's charged with a dolorous current. Herbert Read refers to a "divided nature" that's "tragic" — Leonardo as artist, Leonardo as scientist, meeting like brothers on different sides in the war. In the notebooks "we find feelings and sensations recorded in all their poetic actuality, and these same feelings and sensations converted to idea, coldly analyzed and dissected." And this, says Read, is why Leonardo "lays down precepts which were to corrupt the artistic consciousness of Europe for the next three centuries."

And "a man can be at the same time great and disastrous." Even Leonardo's intense admirer Kenneth Clark records the frustration and folly of a world in halves: "In 1503 he persuaded the Florentine Government — probably the most hard-headed body in Europe — to accept his design for diverting the Arno so that it should no longer enter the sea by Pisa, but in Florentine territory. . . . It is typical of Leonardo's mind that his notes on the subject are, up to a point, quite factual; but that when he comes to the real difficulty, a range of hills, he says simply 'At Serraville I shall cut through'; without the slightest indication how."

From this unreconciled schism, ills by the oodles.

From silliness ("Jokes with which he occupied his time—animals of paste which flew, and a lizard dressed up to look like a dragon . . . no wonder he despaired of ever putting his researches in order.") to blindness ("He overlooked two of the greatest inventions not only of his time but of all time: printing and engraving. . . How did it happen that Leonardo ignored and rejected all this?") to harm ("The majority of his precepts—to painters—are in effect nothing but formulas for . . . the fixation of emotional cliches.").

—And, finally, to a private sadness. He wrote at the foot of a page of "drawings . . . anatomical of the generative functions": *I have wasted my hours*. A late self-portrait in red chalk, with its "nutcracker nose and sharply turned down mouth," shows an old man, "head on his hand, gazing into the distance, with an air of profound melancholy."

Clark says, almost in disbelief, as the particolor flakes spiral down: "The most scientifically minded artist of the Renaissance painted his two great wall paintings with so little science that they almost immediately disintegrated." Disintegrated. And: inside? *Those* pictures? K. R. Eissler: "Leonardo's basic relationship to the world was a traumatic one."

(He hunkers down on the beach, and by the first thin steak-blood-smudge of sunrise, takes his memorandum-book from his belt with his left hand, digs with his right simultaneously for a crust. He jaws it a while. A duck, maybe lost from the marsh reeds, lands; waddles up, like a low-level papal guard, for a crust of the crust. His left hand busy with a scribblestick of graphite: the wings, the rubbery web-weighted legs . . . His blue eyes perfectly still. Perfectly still and accommodating.)

Commentary, though, on this divided mind is itself divided. "For in truth great love is born of great knowledge of the thing loved"—from his *Treatise on Painting*. And of that love, and its parent knowledge, precisely *because of* this generous double direction, much of Leonardo study is, as one would expect, salutation.

"The strong and the soft were equally his province," Wölfflin says, admiring the very sense of apposite pulls that so disturbs other critics. "If he paints a battle, he surpasses all others in the expression of unchained passions and tumultuous movement, yet he can catch the most tender emotion and fix the most fleeting expression. Qualities which seem mutually exclusive are combined in him" most miscibly: "the world revealed itself in all its inexhaustible riches."

So, sure, in that treasure-trove some stones are smoothed, and lustered. "For Leonardo, delight is the role of the young animal . . . the kittens, playing or licking themselves — the kittens he puts everywhere in his sacred subjects, to the great dismay of his pious patrons." And some stones' edges want blood. "Further on . . . there is effort, tension, monstrosity. There is ugliness and unconscious suffering; above all, there is conscious suffering, everywhere."

For de Santillana: "In all of this, there is a beautiful order. There is a logic, the supreme knowledge of the prime mover . . . which was able to allot to all those powers the quality of their effects in the necessary proportion. The universe has no frustration."

To hold it, all. Roger Shattuck discusses "Leonardo's mental organization," quoting Valéry and Freud, and concludes: "The division we have begun to lament publicly between two climates of thinking, scientific and humanistic, between opposed methods of inquiry, cannot be traced to any corresponding division between regions or faculties in the mind. At the origin is unity."

I can't claim he was a happy man. But I'd like to think so. Philipson: "The fascination of Leonardo's personality rests on this fact: that the essence of self-enjoyment is directly related to the interest one takes in the attractions of the rest of the world — in nature as well as in one's own spirit . . . *all* he did was to *enjoy himself*."

And so I return to his labyrinth-ranges that back his famous smiling model with phantasmagoria rampant: they function. "This is no caprice on the part of the artist, but a means of increasing the apparent solidity of the figure. It is an exposition of some of Leonardo's theories concerning the appearance of distant objects . . . and its success is such, that, in the Salon Carré of the Louvre where the *Mona Lisa* hangs, all the neighboring pictures, even those of the seventeenth century, look flat."

(He's come up from the beach. The land rises, it's mountainous now, he's idly knotting a twist of rope picked up from an overturned hull—he loved knots, and this love I'll speak about later. Now, though, he's lost in convolutions. His eyes took a snail from the sand, his mind's reconstructing it into a spiral staircase—we still have the notes. He's searching for stones, for any kinds of stones, he's poking the gullies and crags of the mandala, wandering—even the pit of it, wanting to find out—even the shadow. He's brought a candle.

"Suddenly there arose in me two things, fear and desire—fear because of the menacing dark cave, and desire to see whether there were any miraculous thing within.")

7.

The Reade Zone Medical Center is west along Irving Park, near where the city boxes itself into suburbs. Just the day for it. Classes are over, I'm with Linda, the sky's the color of cream of potato soup. We joke. It's early fall in Chicago, the roadside weeds—when you're far enough west for such rustic touches as weeds—are like old aerials: gray, telescoping, and bent. We even sing a little. What do *we* know, we've never been near a place like it. And Ellen's committed herself. Voluntarily. We say it a few times, *voluntarily*. How bad could it be?

The grounds are immense, and barren except for occasional wads of litter. The wind has room to accumulate force here; in the parking lot we're almost whipped up with a few crumpled handbills and kleenexes. As if the Mayor's afraid the ground itself might gather gale impetuosity and take suddenly off, the buildings are squat red brick. Like paperweights, they hold down the crewcut lawns.

The hall is long, a bilious green. Something sour and something antiseptic court in the air. It's only our first step in, but already at the far end we can see people with a slow stupid shuffle, animal-shouldered, animal-jawed, their blinkless eyes as uniform as their institutional buttons. Even from here we can see, on a few of the faces, anger flash across like bolts of interference slashing a monotone news report. We get closer. These are the orderlies.

We have to sign in. Our names, our relation to patient, the time. As if confessing guilt by association. Then we're frisked. *She committed herself.* The door's unlocked, not without some fussing. *Voluntarily.* It's inches thick and sheeted over in metal. What do *we* know. *Out* is a word a whole panel of doctors has to say.

Well I've seen places like it since. They make you want to drop, like a stone, to a field, and just let the rain hit. With my ex-fiancée I've entered: the floor where you're dragged like a sack; the floor with blood on the walls, and the old people peeing; the Tunnels, in the basement, where there's easy sex, where two eyes full of needing it fall on two eyes empty of everything. Then the medic comes by and says your hearing's postponed. He says don't worry, the guard will be reprimanded. The night is a needle. The day is a night. The guard smiles.

Linda lets me go first. It's a common-room, haphazardly divided by ruptured couches and table-and-chair arrangements. Three dozen people or so, mostly patients, go through their Boschian motions. There's a bunch of frantic pacing, and even the stiller people knit with invisible yarn or pluck at cello-string drool or shake their heads like cans of paint till they hear the metal ball clicking. Ellen stands out by her quietude. She's in a chair by a window, huge as ever, her hands asleep in her lap. A burly redheaded fellow, ringlet-haired and bearded, growls protectively. Warning over, he leaves in a slope-shouldered walk. We sit down. Less a group portrait; more a still life.

"Flipped your coco, huh?"

No answer from Ellen. Her jaw is blue with a coat of stubble. Colorless flowers pattern a shapeless frock.

She's so serene, though. It's hard to be sad. And then her hands lift up, and swirl, like young birds learning.

Slow, very slow: "Albert." And then: "I. felt. a. little. wrong."

We spend a half hour that way. It's disconcerting but never dramatic: Ellen's answers always make sense. They're long in coming, though, as if she's standing back a couple of miles inside herself. And always her hands, her bird-friends, answer first.

Sammy's fine.

They miss you at the office.

What a way to get out of work.

Some great material here.

Do you want your books. Do you want your books. Ellen. Do you want your books.

The window's barred but clean and the light pours in. A few times there's a smile even, clumsily done, as if drawn on her face by a child – in that room, though, it's exemplary mirth and Linda and I hang onto it. We say we'll visit again. On the way home Linda cries. It sounds so healthy, compared to the Center's gibbering. The sky, which for a time had opened up, goes gray again and I drive around a long while, not straight back, in wide consoling automotive circles.

Three dozen people or so, on valium. – Whose mouths are open all day around the *e* in *help* but can't get the *help* out.

8.

"Yellow brick was a common building material in late nineteenth-century architecture." But what Baum does with it! Certain ritual, certain fantasy, pertinent channels of psychic need, allow the common walkways of the world to exhibit on either side (as Eissler says referring to Leonardo's art) "the transcendent through the immanent." By the time Baum's into chapter three, that "hard, yellow roadbed" Dorothy takes will lead us past "neat fences at the side of the road" and "fields of grain and vegetables" to a talking scarecrow, witch trouble, flying monkeys, and a ripping away of the curtain that secrets humbug authority everywhere.

The movie journey is classic. Judy Garland, in a special corset to flatten her breasts, gives splendid authenticity to Dorothy.

Special effects spent a week, picking the proper yellow (in those days some shades photographed green). One-hundred-and-twenty-four Munchkins gather around to the Good Witch Glinda's invitation: "Come out, come out wherever you are / And meet the young lady who fell from a star. / She fell from the sky, she fell very far / And KANSAS she says is the name of the star."

They greet her in all their diminutive flowerpot greasepaint mustachioed pouf-sleeved jester-capped sunbonnet glory. You know what's ahead: the mythic journey: past smudgepot, past axe-head, to brains and courage and heart. But I want to focus in now at the start of it all, the genesis-spot of the Yellow Brick Road: Dorothy's ruby slippers taking the first irreversible steps: it'll straighten, and swoop,and follow both the most bizarre and most pragmatic of narrative needs: but first it begins as a spiral.

* * * *

So, the common walkways of the world. On the floors of old churches, one can still find stylized pilgrimage trails, done in mosaic design with Jerusalem marked out at the center. "These pilgrim-age ways are labyrinths, like that in which Theseus killed the Minotaur. This is clearly spelled out in the church of San Michele in Pavia, where, beside the labyrinth, are the words: *Theseus intravit monstrumque biforme necavit* ('Theseus entered and killed the two-natured monster')." Killed it. Maybe (another way of saying) made it whole.

It isn't strange, by now, to see how many paths partake of the shape — especially those that have to do with spiritual matters, especially those in which the spiritual matters have once been institutionalized. Think of the codified merrymaking swirl about the maypole. Or, austerely but just as ecstatically: the Mevlevi dervishes: turn, and whirl, and turn. "Ancient mazes marked out in turf or with stones are often called after Troy, itself a word apparently meaning 'to turn.' These Troy mazes are connected with dances at places held to be entrances to the other world." For initiation, Australian aborigines are commanded to take to the bush — it's termed a "walkabout," they "wander through the country, hunting as they go, singing and swinging their bullroarers as a mark of their new status," braving the maze of the wilds. "This is why he who knows how to follow or make the diagram has his passport to the other world and resides in the god."

Then it isn't strange that the pagan puzzleway laid out by Daedalus reappears in Christian guise—the floor of Chartres Cathedral "with a pathway some six hundred and fifty feet in length, leading round and about until the center is reached." The French labyrinths "appear to have been called *in lieue* or *Chemin de Jerusalem;* they were placed at the west end of the nave and people made a pilgrimage on their knees."

Nor is it unexpected to find the motif predating Daedalus—the rock carvings in the Camonica Valley, Italy. "A demon is represented . . . as a labyrinth. The legend of the Minotaur doubtless draws its origins from this kind of concept. Sometimes the monster is pictured within the labyrinth; sometimes he seems to be one with it, to be himself the labyrinth."

A thread through human history—with many looped knots up its length, but running uncut, and always connecting.

And those prehistoric rock carvings . . . from where do they draw *their* origins?

A man in Texas wakes, and shivers, and at 3:00 A.M. is the only live thing in the universe. He wants to make it through. He wants to stare it down, till the sun rises and the world starts. He wants to be new. He stares then, hard: his fingerprints, whorl-in-whorl. *TO this, THROUGH this, OUT again.*

"Or, as John Layard has observed, among many similarities in labyrinth ceremonials and beliefs 'certain facts stand out as being of special import.' The rites invariably have to do with 'death and rebirth.'"

* * * *

And so they learn their attributes, through trial, and by way of initiation into this world of new-found knowledge, receive appropriate symbols: a ribboned diploma (he furrows his dirty cloth forehead and quotes the means whereby we formulate the hypotenuse); a ticking heart-shaped watch; a medal stamped HERO. "The men who are broken in body (the Scarecrow, the Tin Woodman) are restored to wholeness, as is the one who is broken in spirit (the Cowardly Lion)."

Dorothy returns to her origin-world, bolstered by her gain: a heightened sense of Self and Place. "In the end, reality and home are restored." Perhaps she slops the pigs now finding oil and water make rainbows anywhere. Few films live as long or as well.

Its thematic concerns are so lightly a part of the whole, and the whole so unselfconsciously jolly, analysis seems at most a violation; and, at least, seems rude. But the delight survives—and supports—interpretation. "The Yellow Brick Road is the path through the chaos, the anchorage to reality like the river in *Huckleberry Finn*."

"*The Wizard of Oz* was published the same year as Freud's *Interpretation of Dreams*."

A man in Texas will wake from a dream, will shiver with it, but finally feel successfully tested.

The trees of the Magic Wood, the witch's glinting-eyed retainers, doors in the Emerald City irrevocably slammed shut, that lush but oh-so-narcotic field of poppies . . . and then the clear light. The morning, being stronger for the night just spent; the morning and morning's clear light.

Though first it takes being there at the center, a common home of common construction: whoosh through the spirals of cyclone.

9.

They don't manufacture new seltzer bottles—not worth it. Each one extant is an antique "and the handsomest bottles of all, pale-blue or sea-green, with delicate, unseamed, tapered lines, were hand-blown sixty years ago at a glass factory in Czechoslovakia. . . . Because of the pressure in a seltzer bottle, and because of a coiled spring in the head," the shape again, exemplary and commanding wonder, "seltzer stays full of fizz until the bottle is practically empty—unlike an opened bottle of club soda." The bubbles in morning light catching fire, rising like magma red and fresh from planetary creation, here and everywhere: a paean to the shape.

Yes it's morning. The helix of a peeled orange on royal blue china. Yes it's night. The needle in a record, the sweet black jazzy spinning-in.

The Archimedean Spiral "is defined as the plane locus of a point moving uniformly along a ray while the ray rotates uniformly around its end point." Huh? "It will thus be traced by a fly crawling radially outward on a turning phonograph record." Yes, of course, there it is. Not that they notice, the jazz having carried them somewhere into their own post-midnight fleshly definition of the shape.

It shines from high. The Spiral Nebula nests in a telescope tonight, like any many-legged insect safe in a secret chute, and keeping to itself an other-than-human brightness. It calls from below. "Many discoveries—not one of them more interesting, to the layman, than this: the dominant direction of coiling of shells of a certain species of Foraminifera, *Globorotalia truncatulinoides,* changes with some chemical or physical change in the water—probably the temperature." I see them, coil-left, then coil-right, like the sleek fastidious chorus-line kick-kick of the millennia.

Amazing, yes? Wherever our stunned sight turns: amazing. "There is, for example, a small plumed worm called Spirorbis." It secretes about itself a tube which is "not much larger than the head of a pin and is wound in a flat, closely coiled spiral of chalky whiteness. The worm lives permanently within the tube," both snaring its food and breathing by means of "delicate and filmy tentacles." —This from Rachel Carson. —There, on the beach, and fitting her morning's diligence to the shape of the chambered nautilus, the Spirula, the knobbed whelk, the moon snail making its gelid way, the lightning whelk, the tulip shell, the pink conch, the horse conch, the embryo of the nudibranch, the umbilicus-shell of the Sundial of Taiwan.

I sing of the "spirals at the Maltese temple of Tarxien" and "those on a stele from one of the Shaft Graves at Mycenae, c. 1650 B.C." I sing it, sweet and jazzy. The spring in a cheap tin wind-up toy's frog-spotted body, powering half-inch hops. The carried curl of an elephant's trunk. The carried curl of an insect proboscis. Maybe the record stops, but still they're making love. At night—they're powering. The metal thread up a screw. The green spring wound in the cotyledons. Cornucopia.

The new spring drives the new year open. My father goes to synagogue, it's *Rosh Hashono* — "The Head of the Year" — and the first thing he does, as prescribed by The Book, as performed by the ancients and handed on down: is coil the black leather strap of *t'fillin* devoutly up his arm. He pulls it tight. He feels his body's bloodthump tested against this sign of his adoration, successfully tested, he closes his eyes. He blesses me. I sing for his spirals. I sing for his phylacteries.

I sing, and I want you to sing, for a couple tonight on the couch, and what they carry: "the chemical messages of inheritance from generation to generation . . . DNA." Bronowski: "a sort of spiral staircase, with the sugars and phosphates holding it like two handrails. . . . It is an instruction, a living mobile to tell the cell how to carry out the processes of life step by step." It's everywhere, and it isn't stopping. Yarn, on a room-sized industrial spindle. The Three Little Pigs' pink curlicue tails. "The airy, spiraling trellis design of this porcelain plate was created in St. Petersburg for the private dinner service of Empress Elizabeth I, about 1760." They're done, or they're in between, he's getting up to turn the record over — she goes for rosé and a corkscrew, and stops, and thinks of the shape. Let's sing to fill the silence. Rings-in-rings of her ravenblack pubic hair.

Two eyes lost like two crazed hares in a thicket: a woman studying scrimshaw.

Rat (like a lonely man's thought) around an experimental maze (like a lonely man's brain convolutions).

The shape, the shape.

It's Leeuwenhoek, over the world's first microscope — able to pay, for the world's first time, attention to the dozenfold spiraling "animalcules," gray torques, in his glistery spit, in the pastes from between his own teeth.

"A proton enters the bubble chamber from the left, then knocks an electron out of an atom (spiral track), and then collides with another proton to create sixteen new particles in the collision process." — A lovely physics, some of its microphotography scattered with coils like the Bahaman sands.

Collision process, renewals between the collision process. — He walks back from the phonograph, she's in his head like a black sweet bar of jazz. Though he stops at the john first. I sing of the shape, I sing and his one gold note in the bowl is accompaniment. "Urine passing through the slit-like urethral opening is emitted in the form of a thin sheet that twists and spirals for approximately 100 to 150 mm (four to six inches)." In this phase, the length of each twist is determined by bladder pressure (velocity), from "9.5 mm (three-eighths of an inch)" to "an increment of almost fifty mm (two inches)." The shape, its poetries and exonerations, its citizenry, the shape and its anguish, its licorice-twist esperanto, its blood down the drain, its snakeshape copper bracelet up a countess's olive-tone arm, the shape, its dialectic, the shape, its lore and its lure and its singings.

This set down in the autumn of 1979 in a spiral-bound notebook.

10.

Ellen is released in a month. Her parents' money buys her halfway time in a private facility, the Fox Grove Rest Home.

"Albert . . . hi!" A grizzlybear hug and a chimp smile. Real talk: would I like a soft drink from the canteen, would I prefer her room or the sunporch. Pointing this out to me, and that.

Compared to the Reade Zone Medical Center, the Home is a luxury spa where butterball girls from wealthy families come to slim. The room is frilly. The roommate's watching TV while her wrist scars heal. Nobody mentions the scars, but we talk about the TV quite a bit. "I can answer three out of four of the game show questions. I'm thinking in terms of career." The orderlies pass the door like laundered sheets on a clothes line. A bud vase sprouts a jonquil. Ellen's poems taped on the wall. "And my folk opera . . . Albert, when I walk on the beach I sing it to the fish!" There's some excitement in the little box: a schoolteacher's won a trip to Paris and cutlery for a dozen. "I'd sing it to the moon but I can't go out at night yet."

A fact she accepts. They're truly helping her here. They've decided it's lopsided chemicals; lithium will work. The days are spent in analytic chats, in searching her proper dosage. Purple capsules and a pleated paper cup. At ten o'clock the floor turns out for Pill Line. There are zombie faces, faces like bags full of cats to be drowned . . . it's still, let's admit it, the funny farm. I've still had to sign in. But this time, this place— for up to an hour—I can sign Ellen out.

The home is at the point of one of those frequent V's in Chicago where a slum and an older wealthy neighborhood meet. One way you wend across the clover-patched grass of a city park, to where Lake Michigan foams like bacon-fat along a strip of sand. But we want hot dogs in steamed buns With Everything On Them To Go, so drive a couple of minutes into a noontime gnarl.

"Albert, stop, look."

There's a man face down on the sidewalk. I pull over sharp. A dozen people, at least, walk by; some step directly over. He's moaning. A little blood leaks from under his nose, and when Ellen lifts his head we see the blood nets it. He smells like a distillery sieved through an old sock.

"Go 'way." The voice of a mean, hurt crow.

"Albert, we have to help him."

He pisses. It picks up the blood, then the whole wet sheet of it slithers its way to the curb.

It's my father's car.

"Go 'way."

"Ellen, no one who lives here stopped." *You absolute turd, you, Goldbarth.* "Maybe they know best." *You little schmuck.*

"But, he's sick."

We prop him between us, Ellen the Queen of Fox Grove Rest and Goldbarth the Little Schmuck. Then dump him in the back seat like a pair of apprentice garbagemen.

"There's a People's Free Clinic somewhere. They mentioned it in the ward."

"Go 'way."

"Where?"

"Well, I heard about it, but I'm not sure where exactly. Close by. We can stop a policeman and ask."

"*Go 'way.*"

"Should I sing him my opera?"

"Um, let's drive around and find it on our own."

By Lawrence and Broadway he's puked.

"If he'll fit through a window, chuck him out."

"Albert . . ."

"Just kidding." Down Sheridan maybe? Down Ainslie? "But Ellen, your hour's almost up."

"Albert, he's *sick*."

Uh-huh.

Three hot dog stands go by. I'm signed responsible for twenty-five minutes of overtime with a runaway lithium loony, when we find the clinic on some block we've done at least twice.

"Doan wanna."

"Up the stairs, come on. I have to see doctors too."

For some reason this convinces him, and the three of us take the stairs with a kind of back-and-forth progress like eating corn on the cob.

Ellen signs him in.

When we're back at Fox Grove after five desperate minutes of speeding, Ellen hums her way up to her floor. Nobody's around. I'm sweating. She does something in between hums to the book. "Let's go for the hot dogs." "11:30" is artfully smudged into 1:30. When in Home, do as the Homans.

"Okay. We can eat them at the lake."

It's so good, seeing her sit on the sand and wave a kosher weenie With Everything On It to punctuate her points.

The lake can really look sludgy. Today it's not so bad, though; when the clouds break open, it's diamonded and torched, and you think with your nostrils. Canada seems to be in the air. Something fresh, from a long way.

"Sing for me, Ellen."

She sings like a poultice. It falls to everything caught with a barb in the palate, and asks to smooth.

She's seen it, she's stared it down with her eyes turned inward, her voice like new skin over a burn. She sings something green and Welsh, and plants it lush by the side of a shanty in central Ohio. She sings from a series of rounds, to be transcribed on Möbius strips, to never end, ever.

Ellen-With-Tilted-Halo-Of-Mustard. "My parents are coming with Sammy this weekend. Albert . . ."

"What?"

"I think it'll be okay."

I think it'll be okay too. And then she tells me something, My-Friend-Ellen-On-Her-Way-Back-From-Halfway, she tells me something special.

II.

This is where I leave Leonardo: on a beach, having figured it out. Having brought a problem of stairs to the shape of a snail, having it answered there.

He's standing at the tideline in his white Rhenish linen and deep-red Florentine cape. The cape falls in folds to his knees; occasionally a rough wave reaches the hem, which is soaked for an inch all around. And so he's encircled, as if in a magic space.

He loved the spiral. He drew "ten spiral staircases round a tower," refined the architecture, measured, chalked it in, a knotty problem. He's idly knotting a twist of twine.

"It is fascinating to note that Leonardo da Vinci in describing his proposals for building new towns makes the point that all stairways in the 'public housing' blocks should be made spiral stairs so as to prevent the sanitary misuse of stair landings." He who dissected the bowel.

In one of his graphics, he places his name at the middlepoint of an intricate hundred-interwoven-knot design "in the same manner as [the names] of various medieval church architects occupied the central points of cathedral labyrinths. The affiliation of such knots to labyrinths is thus clearly established."

I leave him, where the world of land and the world of water sizzle and mix: contented today, a little weary, sure, but content, and watching the first magenta spill of the day on the ocean. He once did a sketch of *Pleasure and Pain*. They're figures of equal size and substance, looking in separate directions but attached a bit above the waist to the same one healthy functioning torso. Which looks as if it's about to take a step, off the page, its four arms in balance.

He never did fly, but he knew where to take his stand.

He steps off the page, this page. Whatever name the monster had, there's only *da Vinci* now calm and assimilatory, declaring shape from the center.

12.

Five-rayed, four-dimensional, golden, hat as — just the index shows the manifold explorations Jung made of the mandala.

It was "the most complete union of opposites that is possible; " it was a "world clock" that "never runs down . . . that revolves eternally like the heavens." It was a fiery wheel "as a concept for wholeness." He cites an alchemical dragon gobbling its own thick tail, a wide-eyed Christ surrounded by evangelical wingbeating beasts, an intricate Navajo sand-painting vortexing vision, an "eight-petalled flower."

"The horoscope is itself a mandala (a clock)." It was "a vision of Paradise . . . seven large spheres each containing seven smaller spheres." It was "the central symbol, constantly renewing itself . . . often pictured as a spider in its web" or "the serpent coiled round the creative point, the egg." It was "a small-scale model or perhaps even a source of space-time." He charts it through 400 patients' dreams.

The presentations, obviously, vary. Their direction, though, is similar, and clarified by others' later research.

Eliade says it's "the Cosmos" given "in miniature" and thus its re-creation is "equivalent to a magical re-creation of the world." When a magician designs it in corn flour at a patient's bed "the patient is immersed in the primordial fullness of life; he is penetrated by the gigantic forces that, *in illo tempore,* made the Creation possible." And it works: "This drawing is preserved until the patient is completely cured."

Or Huxley, on "a process by which a sick man would sleep in the temple of Aesculapius . . . in order to have the dream that would reveal the cause of the disease" — and, that done, the priests could prescribe a cure. "Aesculapius, the god of healing (whose sign was a staff with two snakes twined around it)."

The Aboriginal Rainbow Snake is another spiral — Huxley reproduces a lovely geometricized bark painting. To be swallowed by the snake is to "have been incorporated into a system of knowledge and action that gives a new sense of direction"—to be initiated. Successfully traveling the alimentary coils means a new life of wisdom or ecstasy—you're vomited up "transformed." But "a labyrinth" as Eliade points out "was at once a theater of initiation and a place where the dead were buried," and the rite of initiation was "a passage in which the soul runs the risk of being devoured"—of, using Huxley's version, *not* being vomited up: condemned to the serpent's belly acids.

"The representation of the beyond as the bowels of Mother Earth or the belly of a gigantic monster is only one among the very many images that figure the Other World as a place that can be reached only with the utmost difficulty." The necessary sickness, madness, death. To know it, "able to look the rainbow snake full in its glaring eyes as it swallows him." And then to emerge a shaman, one of those of the tribe who "cure disease, kill enemies by magic, foresee the future, and make rain fall"—life on what Eliade calls "the transcendent plane," what maybe Leonardo called a good day's work. Preceded by a frightening night's self-inventory.

Much of this assumes what Charles Poncé, in *The Game of Wizards,* convincingly argues: that the cosmos is a unified matrix, ordering itself along certain energy fields, and making its ordering principles known through the symbols shared panculturally in the collective unconscious. The spiral is such a symbol for the Dogon, an African tribe in what was once the French Sudan: totality is a "foundation stone on which the earth is created." It's topped by a spinning whorl, and in the Dogon myths, the entire structure descends from the heavens "down the rainbow, in a sevenfold spiral." Huxley continues: "Plato, in *The Republic,* used the same image as the model of the universe, which revolved upon the knees of Necessity, the spindle piercing the earth at its axis, and the rims of the whorl representing the orbits of the sun and the moon, the planets, and the fixed stars.

"Necessity is a goddess—for it is the woman who spins in these cultures. She spins, measures, and cuts the thread of life, which is then woven into the fabric of the body." The spiral holding—the spiral *as*—Existence.

If Poncé is correct when he espouses "the existence of a principle of order underlying the psyche, a principle that has a definite structure and with which the whole of our psychological and biologic constitution may be intimately linked," a "structure of order inherent in the universe, as the base of both physical and psychological realities"—and if it is the nature of the psyche to produce "archetypal symbolism of an impersonal character, more akin to myth," which is expressive of this Wholeness—then, no wonder certain images are ubiquitous, and speak of being Complete, or of being healed toward Completion, or of the terrible fragmentation before the healing takes place.

Poncé, by way of summing up Jung: "After many years of consideration he concluded that in any deep penetration of the unconscious the individual suffers a disorientation of his conscious personality, a decentering." There appears at such times "the psyche's announcement that an attempt is being made at the unconscious level to rearrange and reintegrate those components of the ego that 'break down' or 'fly to pieces.' The visual representation of this psychological process is the mandala."

13.

"I know it sounds crazy"—she's pleased with that—"but all the time I was there, in Reade Zone, I was living inside my Master's Report."

I look stupid.

"Inside my research on Joyce."

I shake my head, but can't tell if it's marking the air with a yes or a no.

"Remember a heavyset guy with red hair?"

"Sort of."

"He was my best friend there. Remember him, curly-bearded and muscled? Every night we stayed up talking. Sometimes we were strapped to our beds, sometimes not. We often stayed up till dawn."

She says all this so nonchalantly, shaping it out of the light beach day with what remains of a hot dog bun.

"Albert, this is what was in my head the whole time: I was trapped in a maze.

"And he was the Minotaur. He was feeding me clues. And every time I figured one out, I took another turn toward the mouth of the maze.

"Until I was healed."

Calling Up

1. *The Light That Hit the World in 1958*

Sky King's niece was Penny. There was a copilot (maybe a nephew? a chum?) named Clipper the first season, then he was dropped. We even remember the name of the ranch, The Flying Crown, with all this kitsch corroborated by "Some Fun Facts" in the liner notes to an album jacket I had as a kid, and have just dug up in a junk shop's sloppy half-price boxes: *Saturday Morning KID'S SHOW Tunes!* But no one remembers the plane's name.

'Melia looks up from her book—a study of paranormal experiences reputed to various literary lives. About an hour ago, as we were hammering down the cast of "Lassie," she recited, from out of whatever achronological level she'd wiffled to, "In my ninth year my father suffered a dream in which Death had appeared to him, as he is commonly painted, and touched him with his Dart. That good man came home, took to his bed and accordingly died" (it's Coleridge speaking). Then she returned to silent reading.

Now she blurts, from her unguessable astral Anywhere, "The *Silver Dart*"—this gives it a kind of oracular authority. But after some noggin-thumping and serious liner notes research, Captain

Midnight turns out to have piloted the *Silver Dart,* to the terror of saboteurs everywhere. Buzz Corry, hero of "Space Patrol," commanded the thirtieth-century rocket *Terra;* with Miss Tonga and Cadet Happy, he defeated the Wild Men of Procyon, Captain Dagger, Mr. Proteus, Mazna the Invisible, and the evilmost Prince Baccarratti. Even the sound of their shoestring budget blastoff is clear: the whine of antique dental machinery.

Sky King's plane's name, though, remains below the dust of thirty years. Our friends go home. I'm jittery; Skyler yawns. We leave the last half-inches of beer in their steins for the night. Some formulaic kissing. Then sleep.

For her; not me. It isn't the plane's name really, keeping me staring all night out the living-room window, trying to read lost words in the stars. I couldn't say *what* it is.

The light that hit the world in 1958 is . . . where? Is out there, somewhere. Light doesn't die. The me who's ten is traveling the galaxies smoother than the best-attended engines of the Space Patrol. In telescopes the wild Procyon scientists scan the far skies with, my father's still alive . . .

I'm looking, cargo-cult-of-one, for that plane. Its freight is simply everything that's happened. If the universe curves, and light in the universe curves, that plane is going to land one day, and my father step out and say "Albie, it's late. Stop thinking your crazy thoughts. Now go to sleep."

2. *Alberts*

On the Wichita State University campus, there's a red brick building you see on your right as soon as you take the main drive — squat, and almost perfectly foursquare, not unlike a lovingly-upkept bunker from World War II. Sometimes I've watched it from farther away — a bouillon cube, ox-red and weakly charged with beef.

This is the original Pizza Hut. Yes, the first one, built on some 600 borrowed bucks and offered successfully, nineteen years after that, to PepsiCo for $300,000. "That was a steal." Maybe. Now it's a stela, of sorts. No chip of pepperoni has been inside this fussily-janitored block for years. Its plaque reads:

> PIZZA HUT NUMBER ONE
> FIRST OPENED AT BLUFF AND KELLOGG STREETS
> JUNE 15, 1958
> The building was moved to this site to serve as a symbol and reminder to our students how young individuals through hard work and initiative can still rise from modest beginnings to positions of leadership and success.

We laugh at it, of course. "I'm trying to write about it," I say to Skyler. "Do you think I could say it's architecturally . . . you know, a bungalow?" She says, "It's a low bungle." — That kind of thing.

On the second of August, 1939, a letter was sent to President Roosevelt from Old Grove Road on Nassau Point, Long Island, "This new phenomenon would also lead to the construction of bombs . . . powerful bombs of a new type," Einstein said, suggesting funds to "speed up work being done within the budgets of University laboratories." So there's another plaque I've seen — you know, the squash court, West Stands, Stagg Field, University of Chicago:

> ON DECEMBER 2, 1942
> MAN ACHIEVED HERE
> THE FIRST SELF-SUSTAINING CHAIN REACTION
> AND THEREBY INITIATED THE
> CONTROLLED RELEASE OF NUCLEAR ENERGY

though laughing at that's less easy.

We commemorate. *Homo historical marker,* that's us. Off Highway 71 near Audubon, Iowa, a sizeable chunk of sky is covered by Albert, "The World's Largest Bull," concrete and steel measuring thirty feet tall by fifteen wide "at the horns," all painted credibly enough in buff and umber. He weighs in at forty-five tons. His balls hang down like a punching bag of the gods. He's not forgettable; but, just in case, there's postcards.

We commemorate, we love to, I suppose we need to — evidently too much hubbub-ballyhooed accomplishment occurs to trust the brain unaided. If we don't find plaques, we don't find the concept of history altogether. "Where there was so little difference between past and present" (Daniel Boorstin is writing of ancient India) "the quest for history seemed futile. In a society that did not know change, what was there for historians to write about?"

You stumble over fire in a world that's never known it, say a lightning-gutted oak: that place is sacred, is recorded in scratched antler-bone as sacred. But enormous successions of hunter-gatherer generations must have passed without such singularity. Time was a life, your own life; everything else was a cycle. Monuments have no place in a cycle. Myth is round; nostalgia exists on a line.

And yes: if too much too-eventful stuff has intervened, why, I can look up Albert on one of his postcards.

Yes, or this one—reproducing a painting by Zeljko Premerl. Einstein in the desert. A turtle is cupped in his hand, a turtle *that* small. Its neck's exposed, an inch of nuzzle against the soft round of the physicist's palm: it trusts him. Its shell is glowing, as if from within; the lines between the burls give it the look of a Tiffany lamp the size of a doorknob.

Einstein sits on a throne fit together from bones—or, more exactly, it's the skeleton of a giant Galapagos tortoise. All around is sand, then mountains in the background, and a missile: red-tipped, itchy to launch. Essentially, the scientist is mediating between the small life and the monstrous devastation. He isn't happy for this: his face pulls at the corners of his eyes. His whole face, weighted with his knowledge.

The painting's dated 1976 — it's thirty-seven years since his letter. He hasn't forgotten, though, or left his post. It's why he's here: he's a sign. He won't let us forget, either.

3. *Part One, with Ratchets*

In early March I visited 'Melia's hospital room. The clot lodged in a lung this time. For someone only thirty-five who'd stared at death through the width of a strand of fibrinogen or less, she was incredibly much her bellicose gutsy self—by this time, surgery was decided against, and she was "simply" waiting for the thinners to unclog her chest, and working at not wondering where the clot would declare itself next time, and when.

As always, her courage astounded me—humbled me, more accurately. We made some standard chatter. I did unnecessarily nasty imitations of my colleagues, 'Melia was equally wicked with medical horror stories: a surgeon who'd accidentally sparked a patient's bowel gas and was blown across the room. And: "Did anyone ever remember the plane's name?"

"Not yet." Catching glimpses of the lei of internal bleeding across her breast. "Say, what were you working on?"

"Before this?"

"Yeah. Before this."

'Melia's . . . interesting. "Before this" she was doing a series of former lovers in clay. "It got more serious, but first I was going to have them with their pants around their ankles. From a Coleridge line I picked up in that book. 'As if this earth in fast thick pants were breathing.' " (Laughs) "That's what I was going to title the series: *Fast Thick Pants*."

A TV's set in the wall. One channel is totally oldies, and when Pizza Hut's done flaunting a medium "sausage-supreme" with the weight of a lead gong, eerily familiar music mists into the room . . . "The Time Tunnel."

Each week Doug and Tony, blandly handsome Hollywood-version scientist he-men, entered their spiral-hypnotic Tunnel (part of Project Tic-Toc) and exited into some past or future Earth. The Vikings. Space invaders. You-name-it. Now 'Melia and I stare fixedly, as if through invisible surveyor's tripods or rifle sites, down twenty years of time-gone-by. "Reruns," she says to me, "reruns. They're like ratchets dragging you backwards."

This one, Doug and Tony need to find a certain common yard bird in the past and relocate it in the future. Something like that. The bird's become the focus of "a shift in cosmic vectors," a kind of fluffy foundation stone for the building of all of sequential time, and the fate of the planet (*ho hum*—once again, for Doug and Tony) hangs in the balance. It's a two-part story. Part one done, an oldies rock show hoarsely do-ron-rons from the speaker.

"I'd better get ronning myself. Skyler sends this:" (A-kiss-to-her-cheek).

An oldie, "Cherish," shoo-bops in my mind the full way out of the hospital warren, getting lost, redoubling, opening up wrong doors, the song containing entire people inside it, things that happened, intact, and then a room of jars with organs pickled in alcohol floating whole that same way. Brains. A heart.

4. *Scattered Bodies*

For weeks I was jealous of 'Melia's clay figures. I *also* wanted emptying out the vacuum cleaner bag of love, to sort with picky relish through its gleanings, maybe golemize those bits somewhat, and by spirit and sputum refashion a mannequin Ellen, Morgan, Claudia, who would crackle with the living static of yesterday. I'd think of 'Melia over her unformed lumps of it as a sorceress able to call up, even if semblanced only, the dead.

But I can't work clay, and no litany I tried — their charms, their brokenness, their various smiles and storm-warnings — worked much better. I could "call up" my old lovers, yes, by phone: if they had phones, and were listed, and kept their same names, if the decades are wired underground for long distance. But that was the only call-up conjuring I felt capable of, a tepid one at that, and resisting its urges wasn't difficult.

I *can't* deny, though, the sooty woo of a junk shop. Pages wearing their foxing as lush as stoles, paint-scaled lawn jockeys grouped like a leper colony's Christmas carolers, Persian lamb and Spanish fly, tin condom cases, a homemade lute with a varnish so flypaper-rich you'd swear its maker's face was gummed in its surface retrievably all these years . . . I'll dive into such detritus with the fervor Schliemann, Leakey, Dr. Frankenstein, Vesalius, and Don Juan brought to their bodies of work.

A gimp, one-runnered rocking chair. An advent calendar — tiny doors flung wide like the raincoats of flashers. Strands of pearls. A fishbowl of matchbooks, of pop bottle caps, of rubber sardines. I'm hooked, I'm looking. Somebody — many somebodies—forgot these things, these once-dear things, and I'm excavating the cluttered underside of their amnesia.

Limpid confirmation tresses, in their vellum binder. Here: a ratty raspberry velveteen-covered wedding register of guests' best wishes in fading tea-stain ink. This basin of sturdy eggnog glazeware, missing its pitcher. These crystal knobs. Fletched Pawnee ceremonial headgear on its side like a roadkill. Three original 1936 Mickey Mouse alphabet blocks that can't spell anything, in any combination, except for the nonsense gutturals damage always utters. This is one port in solidity's diaspora.

John Donne, that man whose mind was filled by numinous beings in strict theological order, says that one day we will all be resurrected, wired entire again, each tooth a bar fight batted out, each ovary snipped from its system: back, and functioning, and humming in well-oiled pleasure. He tells the angels, "Blow your trumpets," and "Arise from death, you numberless infinities of souls, and to your scattered bodies go." It may seem, waiting in his grave for close to four centuries now, that only an eyelash-flicker of chronology has passed. It may. I have my doubts. But John Donne has his faith. Right now, his eyelashes may be soaking in the nutrient-troughs of some deific escrow, held there incorruptible waiting for the signal to follow their chromosomal maps of the cosmos back home.

Those confirmation tresses: will they, that day, tremble in the seizure of being sparked in their cells? I have my doubts. But, still . . . That half-bald wedding book, where half of backlands Kansas seems to have scribbled its wishes one moth-brown day in 1886, *Ma Saw and Brother Snitched / So now the two of you is Hitched* . . . Do objects people loved return to life when those who loved them do? Donne's mum on this. The physics of it is unknown.

What Boschian miracle-scene will it be like, caught on Rapture Day in rows of junk shop rupture, when the fiddle necks and two-penny nails and wristwatch straps and anchor chains are called to completion, stir, then whisk the air with their sudden ascension? Every Russian Easter egg and whorehouse parlor piano slamming its long-dispersed constituent slivers to Oneness seamlessly, and rising . . . The physics of this is wholly unknown in a universe where the condition of anything being itself is: we're flying apart.

Every minute we're entropy's playthings. Boards warp. Hair thins. Rust spreads like a living map of Alexander's advance in a movie. I'm going to walk the unkempt junktique rows, and call up every love that's brushed against these objects in the days of their utility, call up into light against the grain of time. Plate silver. A pair of jade gods. Fiestaware. A much-smudged Captain Midnight mug. The thumbling netsukes. A spare but sinuous-silhouetted Shaker chair. These toucan salt-and-pepper shakers. A fifteenth-century copper filigree Turkish inkstand. Some old admiral's scrimshaw pipe, with stand. Ceramic mermaids. Cranberryware. A taxidermied otter. Valentines. Chamberpots. Butter churns. Tea balls. Humidors. Hair nets. "Press-Rite" collar stays. This deck of cards with tiger-pattern-negligee'd demoness showgirls saying 1958 will never come again . . .

Each time we save one, we apply a brake to the boneshaking speed at which our latticework dismantles.

This is breathy rhetoric, yes. Look, let's get dirty in a corner box, specific. In this carton here, in January 1988, I persevered until I turned up *Saturday Morning KID'S SHOW Tunes!* and it was 1958 I hummed out into.

5. *At Night in a Room by Simonides*

I implied that Einstein wrote a letter to Roosevelt, encouraging the funding of atomic research.

Einstein typed that letter and signed it; the text was Leo Szilard's.

Less well-known than the hero who squared MC for the world, still it was Szilard, Hungarian émigré in London, who—supposedly at a red light, waiting green—"realized that if you hit an atom with one neutron, and it happens to break up and release two, then you would have a chain reaction." He filed a patent containing the phrase in 1934.

Well, that's how memory works for most of us. From everything, from *reverie-thing,* from all of this colliding—I'm ten. It's 1958, I'm in a hospital bed.

The pain's not major. The frightening apparatus, though—so reminiscent of dungeon torture, devices the vile scientists of Procyon contrapted with hooks and blades—has had my muscles almost epileptically stampeding at times. The room smells *too* clean, *stinks* of "clean"—they're covering something up. Long animal screams with human names or God's attached eke through the walls. The day before, an eighty-year-old woman, Mrs. Kreitzer, her intestine hanging out her rectum, maundered down the hall. Three decades later, and her name is as clear as the *Bic* on the pen I'm writing this with: Kreitzer, Mrs. Kreitzer.

Thirty years, and I can see each line of helplessness ordealed in my parents' faces. Some I helped engrave myself—as if *they* were responsible for the invisible machinations of germs. In 1958 we lived next door to Vito's Pizza; Vito couldn't "speeka Eengle" but his gooily voluptuous goods communicated panculturally in straight talk to the tongue, and these I craved, and they were all I needed as weekly reward for good conduct.

So the more the Chief Nurse said that any "outside food" was outlawed, the greater I whined, the more I intuitively knew to ply the idea my "favorite," my "special," food was what I needed, what my parents surely understood in a mystic familial way that I needed, to speed and even to seal as completed, my recovery. They were miserable, I was heartless. The Nurse's lizard-eyed Procyon minions kept stern watch.

Finally, in fact, my parents argued. I'd heard this before in minor ways. "Let's heat it up." "You're nuts, it's always better cold the next day." "Why spend money on that?" "On *that?* Well if you really want to know a thing or two . . ." But never in front of me, like this, with a slap. I can hear it right now. After all, it's my fault.

She ran wild from the room, and it was my fault. He offered one weak smile of "it's alright" that rode his face like light on what you knew was miles of murky water, and it was my fault and he walked out crisply—spoke to me some last consoling father-stuff, then walked out with the pieces of the day in his hands—and it was my fault. As if the shots, the ether mask, and the IV needle weren't enough.

Now I could tell you in detail every object in that room. The terrible energy in not sleeping will devote itself to the round of a glass, to the infinitesimal nuances of dark or daybreak, with equally terrible clarity. I was awake and suffering: no individual dot in the ceiling's soundproofing panels escaped my notice.

The classical "architectural technique" for improving the memory, as devised by Quintilian and basing it on Simonides of Ceos, was "to think of a building; and study its rooms; and deposit in each an image that will concretize the idea you wish to remember." This was *the* pre-Gutenbergian wisdom. Students of rhetoric would find a deserted building and methodically attend to the minutiae of each corner and sill, attempting to warehouse their consciousness.

The glass is three-fourths filled. My lips are sticky from my system's bout with crisis, and they've left two imprints, gray slugs, on the rim. The water's gray, too, in that last of the sun, and eventually the final flex of sunset gilds the surface of the water—when disturbed, this gold compacts itself to a wavery crown in the center—but soon the whole room's dark and the water transparent. Even so, a night-light gives the sides of the glass a powdery definition . . .

Every object. And my father's voice, its useless consolation remaining. "Albie, it's late. Stop thinking your crazy thoughts. Now go to sleep."

6. *Brains. A Heart.*

I don't want this melodramatic. My parents found each other. Originally, sure: that full moon shirred by clouds, and when they'd reached the center of Humboldt Park Lagoon he threw both oars overboard and asked would she marry him. That's a family legend. The moon! The stars! But now I mean only this: their mutual radar was working, and at Pete's Eats—a cafeteria not one block away from the frenzied hospital main entrance—they met, conferring into reconciliation.

I don't want this impossibly mystical either. They found each other, why not? Bonds form in over a score of years of intimate knowing; maybe some bonds pre-exist us; and we hear our names called out, through an invisible rail our ear is against, and we hearken. If it happens in a minor key—my near hand opens up and Skyler, deep asleep still, curls her hand inside it as assuredly as if her hand could see — some major moments are on record.

This is what 'Melia's been reading, in writers' lives.

Was it with anger, tears, or her rehearsed flirtatious sliding of a ribbon back and forth across her nipples that he loved to watch so much, that Anne implored him to stay? I simplify it. All three, likely, and sturdy attempts at reason. She was pregnant, and unduly weak. France never seemed so far. But he was in casual debt to Sir Robert; the journey, as proposed, was but two months; he tied the ribbon near her nape, in that intricate Chinese skein she always requested his nimble fingers crisscross up her hair . . . "Within a few days after this resolve, the Ambassador, Sir Robert, and Mr. Donne, left London; and were the twelfth day got all safe to Paris."

This is from Izaak Walton (surely I can't improve on his version):

> "Two days after their arrival there, Mr. Donne was left alone in that room in which Sir Robert, he, and some other friends had dined together. To this place Sir Robert returned within half an hour; and as he left, so he found, Mr. Donne alone; but in such an ecstasy, and so altered as to his looks, as amazed Sir Robert to behold him; insomuch that he earnestly desired Mr. Donne to declare what had befallen him in the short time of his absence. To which Mr. Donne did at last say 'I have seen a dreadful vision since I saw you: I have seen my dear wife pass twice by me through this room, with her hair hanging about her shoulders, and a dead child in her arms: this I have seen since I saw you.'
>
> "To which Sir Robert replied, 'Sure, sir, you have slept since I saw you; and this is the result of some melancholy dream, which I desire you to forget, for you are now awake.' To which Mr. Donne's reply was: 'I cannot be surer that I now live than that I have not slept since I saw you: and am as sure that at her second appearing she stopped and looked me in the face, and vanished.'

> "It is truly said that desire and doubt have no rest; and it proved so with Sir Robert, for he immediately sent a servant to Drewry House, with a charge to hasten back and bring him word. The twelfth day the messenger returned with this account: — That he found and left Mrs. Donne very sad and sick in her bed; and that, after a long and dangerous labor, she had been delivered of a dead child. And, upon examination, this circumstance proved to be the same day, and about the very hour, that Mr. Donne affirmed he saw her pass by in his chamber."

Pages later, Shelley's dead.

The sea salt lines his lungs; you could crack them over your knees. According to Trelawny, the corpse is stained "a ghastly indigo." Then: "more wine was poured over Shelley's body than he had consumed during life. This with the oil and salt made the yellow flames glisten and quiver." Sea wind feeding the fire. Gulls above like paid mourners.

Byron, even, needs to look away. "The frontal bone of the skull fell off; and, as the back of the head rested on the red-hot bottom bars of the furnace, the brains literally seethed, bubbled, and boiled as if in a cauldron."

"The heart remained entire." Trelawny snatches it out of the cracklings. "I collected the ashes. . . . Byron and Hunt retraced their steps to their home . . . ."

There's a tale: Mary Shelley would unlock the heart from its vanity table case. It looked japanned now. In her grief she would hold it and concentrate. There is no physics to measure grief. There is no proper history to the short wave radio set. In her grief, in the swaddled-up night. "There is an account she would call him; or *recall* him, this is what it would have been. Betimes, he would answer. She would witness him writing, or stomping in a writer's frustration again about the room." In her grief, at her bedside. "She would feel the touch of his palm at her breast, as truly as if they leaned against a column of the villa and the moon on her bone buttons was a calendar of moons he was, by one at a time, undoing."

7. Part Two, with Presents

Nor did melodrama play a part in 'Melia's recovery. Overnight the clot became the wisp of a clot, and though her blood now was nearly as thin as water, she was ready for home.

I visited her room a few hours prior to checkout. I'm the troglodytish type that doesn't own a TV—but I wanted to see how Doug and Tony were managing their travails. First, an oldies "Horror Review" devoted to 1950s Japanese monsters: Mothra, Rodan, Godzilla (the *rex* of them all), and various lesser-known clones, was each in turn destroying downtown Tokyo. Fires broke out. Ninety-story buildings crumbled like dry cake. Dorms full of coeds were caught with nothing but bath towels betokening modesty.

"Y'know, there's something less than full credibility here."

"You're crazy—that's a twelve-yard stretch of saliva in those jaws and you don't *believe* it?"

"Do I look scared?"

"You've just got rid of an Unidentified Flying Clot in your body—of course *you're* not scared. You're not a fit audience."

"Sure but—"

"Ssh."

It's night and they're crawling through savage landscape, sneaking toward a camp of clearly evil human beings, or maybe not even human beings: ape-faced proto-men, perhaps, or extraterrestrials. In any case, the campfire dances maniacally over blunt features. Why would our scientist buddies care to risk their moussed-down suavity, tangling with this foul crew? Easy: on a flat rock in front of the chief of this Hun-like consortium, there's a superduper far-future cage, and in it: something fluttering, warbling.

All of time, down to the first amoeboid cytoplasm-sex, and up to who-knows-what ecstatic court-and-spark on farflung planets, is at stake. There's tussling, running, brief soliloquies on being brave, the piling-up of adversity, shouts, the cage itself and its avian occupant thrown in the long high arc of a football play . . . I don't remember it all and, anyway, before the final scene, an orderly interrupted: the office was ready for checkout.

Doug to Tony, a long high stadium-rousing epochs-hopeful pass—or Tony to Doug . . . the rest, I can imagine.

. . . as I've had to imagine patches into the fabric of that other hospital scene. Our memories never are perfect. This is what I see:

They make a gala entrance into my room that following morning. They're holding hands. They've brought presents—even presents (gimmicked-up memo pads) for the nurses, even the Chief Nurse, she of the vigilant scowl. "How ya doin', Professor!" (Ten years old, and he called me Professor.) It's no question, but an assertion of vim. Whatever nightlong patchwork they've done to *their* emotional fabric, its thread is bright gold in this otherwise-lusterless setting.

All their bluster beamed, sublingually, "Everything's okay now," with its subspeech subtext, "Everything was never *not* okay—right?" (This is my earliest understanding of the endless assault revisionist history aims at personal memory.) A lot was at stake in that hearty "right?" Would I be sweetly conned? (This is one of my earliest understandings of power.) For minutes there, in antiseptic no-space, *they* were the children, simpering, scheming, naked in intention, and my word would hurt or heal.

So I bought their line; we all hugged. One of my presents was a tin wind-up turtle ("Turtley," I dubbed him: I had no knack at names); his spring was durable enough so that his waddling progress took him the length of the wheeled bedside stand. The second present was strange, an album jacket, *Saturday Morning KID'S SHOW Tunes!*—there was no record player in the room.

But then, there was no record in the jacket.

My father kept watch at the door, his arms crossed. "Good morning," I'd hear him repeat. And I pulled out a small but exemplary wheel of Vito's mushroom-and-double-cheese.

"It's always better cold the next day," my father said over his shoulder.

"Your father's a nut case," she told me, laughing.

8. *Photo-Graph*

Light doesn't die. Its source might — not the light. We know now, *any* star we see, we see at the end of a beam of light that's Time-Tunneling space. And if we see a star that's dead, by its continuously residual light . . . well, here's the picture my mother snapped at the hospital exit: I'm waving good-bye and he's holding me, his exuberant package, with clumsy affection while both of us squint in the sun.

Light doesn't die; we *can* call up. It's the commonest scientific wisdom of twentieth-century poems, repeated in hyperimaginative contexts like this one until it accumulates spiritual force: the past can be grabbed by its photoelectron lapels and dragged into immediacy. "The North American Hopis see time in terms of events rather than of units. Their language avoids our confusion with past and future, by putting everything in an elaborate and subtle multiplication of the present."

It's one big calling-up world out there. Throughout the early 1940's Stefan Ossowiecki, an elderly Pole, "a chemical engineer with no conscious interest in prehistoric archaeology," was subject of a number of impressive tests at the University of Warsaw. Listen: for twenty minutes, he's been clasping a small and seemingly insignificant stone, and now he speaks: *I see very well, it is part of a spear . . . I see round houses, wooden, covered with gray clay, over walls of animal hide . . . People with black hair, enormous feet, large hands, eyes deeply set . . .* "He went on for an hour, giving a detailed view of the daily life, dress, appearance and behavior of a Paleolithic people," although Ossowiecki himself had no idea to which specific period scientists already dated the stone.

Until his death in 1944, he was tested with thirty-two objects out of the Warsaw Museum — Acheulian, Mousterian, Aurignacian, Neanderthal, up to the present day. "[Although] these accounts were stimulated by objects that only experts could be sure to recognize . . . his descriptions are not only consistent with what was then known about the cultures in question, but sometimes included information that has only come to light as a result of discoveries made since he died."

The same proof-after-the-fact validates truck driver George McMullen, "who has no formal education and never reads anthropological literature." Discovered by Professor of Archaeology Norman Emerson, McMullen has been repeatedly asked to bring his expertise to field expeditions, pacing the area, stiffening, hackled, describing the people who lived there—age, dress, rituals, buildings. "He once walked over a patch of bare ground, pacing out the perimeter of what he claimed was an Iroquois long-house, while Emerson followed behind him placing survey pegs in the earth. Six weeks later, the entire structure was excavated exactly where McMullen said it would be."

Eyes closed, holding the stone—the same as (though the opposite from) a gypsy over her crystal ball with the future therein. Eyes closed, and seeing. Calling up.

Tierake! Teirake! (Arise! Arise!)—the by-now-ethnographically-famous South Pacific porpoise callers: specifically, "of the High Chiefs of Butaritari and Makin-Meang." They claim their spirits dream-travel under the western waters and, there, invite the porpoise-folk into the world of people. Arthur Grimble witnessed the leading caller of Kuma rush from his hut after several hours of silence, fall face-down to the sands, then amazingly leap up "clawing at the air and whining." The porpoises had arrived.

"They were moving towards us in extended order with spaces of two or three yards between them, as far as my eye could reach. So slowly they came, they seemed to be hung in a trance. Their leader drifted in hard by the dreamer's legs. He turned without a word to walk beside it."

The sun along each of those elegant silver-blue backs. The villagers stooping to ease them over the ridges, crooning. More each minute. Responding. Called up.

And the family dogs that appear at the door after 500 trotted miles of foreign terrain. The spectral visit of lover to lover, mother to daughter, sometimes cities distant, sometimes over an ocean, in crisis-excitement. Gossip-fodder oddities on their own, somehow persuasive in mass, these stories exist indeed in mass, and shelving them under "Paranormal" won't belie the weight of their compelling, crackpot evidence.

Or gospel: *Operator, Operator, Get me Jesus on the line.* We need to call up. A ghostly child the size of a thimble can stand at the ears of the men and women of my generation and plaintively yell to the deeps of their half-sleep haze, *Oh Laaasie, LAAASIE*—the collie never fails to come, from wherever she's been in the brain's back brambles, her theme music faintly trailing. Junk shops are memorabilia emporia, outpouring this century's souvenir postcards, autograph books, memento pins and badges, keepsake lockets, Kodak albums . . .

Here, my father's alive, I'm waving good-bye to the camera. The sun of a single day of 1958 is something elusive, fixative, intimate, impenetrable, alien, is particles, is waves. My mother's included here too—her blur of thumb.

In English, it means "light-image" of course. In Hopi, I'm also waving hello.

9. *Mushrooms*

And this is a photograph too: On the steps of the Sumitomo Bank, the heat and light of the atomic bomb imprinted a man's crumpled shadow. "The steps have been left as a reminder—after a nuclear blast, only the shadow of a man remains, a shadow in the stone."

And this is the final stitch of Leo Szilard's threading through my thoughts:

"When in 1945 the European war had been won, and Szilard realized that the bomb was now about to be used on the Japanese, he marshalled protest everywhere he could. . . . He wanted the bomb to be tested openly so that the Japanese should know its power and could surrender before people died. As you know, Szilard failed."

And this is the testimony of humankind's failure; these are recollections, thirty years later, of hibakusha, *explosion-effected-ones," Hiroshima's survivors:*

"I was horrified at the sight of a man standing in the rain with his eyeball in his palm. There was nothing I could do for him."

"A woman with her jaw missing and her tongue hanging out of her mouth was wandering around the area of Shinsho-machi in the heavy, black rain."

"I was too shocked to feel loneliness for my husband. It was like hell. A living horse was burning."

"A woman under a concrete block, 'Please help me.' Four or five of us tried, but we couldn't move the block off her. What to do? We said 'Forgive us' and walked away. . . . Another lady, the blood was oozing from the corners of her eyes. My mother, the skin of her hands was hanging loose, as if it were rubber gloves. My father, disappeared. We never even found his body."

"Then I heard a girl's voice from behind a tree. 'Help me, please.' Her back was completely burned and the skin peeled off and was hanging down from her hips."

"There was a charred body of a woman standing frozen in a running posture with one leg lifted, and clutching her charred baby in her arms."

"The girl was alive and maggots crawled in and out of her body, but she was too weak to trouble with that. They tried applying oil and seaweed, but later she died."

"The sky was red. The sky was burning. Above the city was the mushroom cloud."

And this is how the world reacts, and how the world's always reacted:

"When Simonides offered to teach the Athenian statesman Themistocles the art of Memory, Cicero reports that he refused. 'Teach me not the art of remembering,' he said, 'but the art of forgetting, for I remember things I do not wish to remember, but I cannot forget things I wish to forget.'"

And these are the children of hibakusha:

"Our generation does not like to talk about our fears. We consider them taboo. It is better to talk about ordinary things." *— He talks continually about mahjongg, which he loves to play all night.*

"I never think about what happened here. When I am finished with work, I bowl, go to bars and the movies. I want to have a good time."

"Everyone in Hiroshima faces this problem — how much to remember, how much to forget."

And this is how we remember:

At the Peace Museum, objects themselves — metal, rock, stones, tile, glass — are as eloquent as the human survivors. More so, even: they never halt their story. "These objects were gathered right from the burning ruins by a geologist."

"He even collected shadows."

In the year before the *Enola Gay* dropped its monstrous atomic payload, Stefan Ossowiecki was murdered, one of millions, by the Gestapo. Where's *his* shadow? Now who's going to rummage the cornermost cartons and find his skull, and tune it in like a receiving device, as he did? Who's going to be the mouth for that bone jaw, and testify?

And why are these ghosts upwelling over the slightest of arbitrarily-reminiscent cues in my portrait? — Einstein sorrowfully cupping his turtle . . . Albert winding his tin one up . . . *Albert with Mushrooms in Hospital* (medium: *memory*; dated: 1958).

On the way out, 'Melia tells me, "All of those clomping Japanese movie monsters, those iguana-things about the size of Rhode Island — they were created by radiation, an atomic explosion or leak or whatever. They keep on returning. They won't let the country go. They won't let those people forget it."

10. *Chain Reaction and* — Sssh!

For months I woke with nightmares.

To whichever one of them fumbled from bed with the comforting word and shoulders-stroke, I'm sure I'd describe — part shamed for having been its recipient, part in fascination with its credible grotesqueries — some jumbled tale of tentacled Procyon-beings chasing me, roping me down. I'm just as sure now they were doctors and nurses, stored in whatever battery a ten-year-old has, for the necessary repressions by which we get through; stored, and transformed; and released, in the brain's own willy-nilly time, as jolts of fang-creature evil.

Days were otherwise. Whatever peril awaited me in the sunlight, it was sized to an understandable world: an older kid could pick on you, a dumb remark of your parents in public could cause the deepest stain of humiliation. But mostly I see those days of my childhood as nurturing and calm — my life is lucky this way — and when I stepped into the courtyard with my khaki-color plastic soldiers, or with that hollow high-bounce ball my peer group called a "pinky," the Chicago sun would fold around me (even in winter, even bundled cumbrously against snow) with that relaxing and utterly *there*-sense of a warm, fresh-laundered flannel-something snugged up to my cheek.

And at night, in bed, in the minutes before they'd come to flick the light switch off, I'd survey my room with intuitive grasp of those same architectural-based mnemonics Simonides formulated. To the grain of the headboard (now a jungle) I'd assign Flash Gordon. Tarzan, ready to leap to my aid, perched ever-wary on a dresser knob. Aquaman, the water-breathing warrior of the briny deep, on my desk. Gene Autry. Rin-Tin-Tin. I had dozens of cardinal points, and equal dozens of chosen protectors. Whatever these figures meant to my friends then, they're the trivia stuffs of our nostalgia now, the once-upon-a-time by which an adult generation comes to recognize its hidden members.

Last year, when Skyler came home from her week in the hospital—home, from her spine and its nerves having reached an uneasy accord—I saw her grown-up's version of those after-effects. She was afraid, the way we all are after being depersonalized and pained while tied. Some nights, that whole week fit in dark minutes. I needed to hold her. Sex wasn't the point. She needed to feel being herself again, in a known and controllable space.

Holding this woman I love, I was them, I was me when they heard my first panicky calling and flung on the cheap terry bathrobe and brisked to my room. "Albie . . ." (piqued a little) "sssh . . ." (pure comfort, that; it came with a long back-stroking glissando) ". . . sssh."

I'd seen them do it for each other too. "Oh, Irv," she'd say, in a sigh that floated the centuries' caring ethereally, through time, through her, and into the kitchen. Or: "Faygeleh," he'd say over and over, rubbing her shoulder as if it might shine. That was the nickname he'd use for those moments. "Faygeleh," he'd say, *"little bird" . . . /*

/ . . . "Doug!" A high one, arcing, arcing . . . "Yo, Tony!" Catching it, cage whole, crazy flapping inside it, and running toward the Tunnel mouth, into it, out of it, breathless, undoing the cage door and holding that rapid chickpea-of-a-heart a second, here at the proper coordinates, petting it, letting it go, the world saved (*ho hum* — once again, for Doug and Tony), the theme music swelling, the title roll, watching the bird grow small against the word TIME and then vanish . . ./

/. . . it was a miniature key; sprites might have forged it. But then, the case itself wasn't even as large as a family Bible. She unlocked it, she'd noticed, especially on nights like this: she'd spent the day alone, and now the moon through some atmospheric effect or another had layered her room in nacre. There: his heart. She lifted it out of its silks. It was dried by now to the size of a child's fist.

She knew what they said: that she imagined she commanded him to appear from Beyond, and the like. But they were damnable fools, possessed of little more than chicken's wits.

She closes her eyes. And when she opens them, *his* eyes are closed, in thought, above a blotted page, the way she best likes to envision him, working, thoroughly absorbed and, so, blind even to her close scrutiny, crossing another word into oblivion, muttering, humming now like a struck tuning fork. His hair is as wild as weeds. He might be writing *To a Skylark* . . ./

/. . . The *Songbird*."

It's been so confusingly long since the question, not one of us recognizes its answer. We're just a bunch of sloshy old friends sitting over some beers at 'Melia's.

"The *Songbird*," she says. She's sure this time. Yes. "Sky King's plane was the *Songbird*."

* * * *

On a Sunday, campus is close to completely empty. In straight sun, the Pizza Hut's ruddy brick glistens. From far off, it catches the light like a polished mahogany shoe. Up close, if you touch it, the building seems to generate animal heat of its own.

When I was a child I'd sometimes go to the closed-in back court sidewalks and, if nobody else was around, I'd stretch out belly-down, my cheek against the concrete. All morning, the sidewalks were storing up sun. That sweetish warmth washed into me, a kind of presexual pleasure that melted my groin, and from there let a tree of warmth branch through me. Finally it curled my toes. It filled me everywhere. I lay there like a pupa of light.

Even at evening's start, the warmth stayed stored there in the concrete. The Earth remembered the sun. When I was a child, the Earth would whisper those memories, whisper its deepest secrets, confidingly into my body.

The Space

I.

This is from when Eric still played with The Rhythm Rangers.

One night, in the lees of the night, when the show was over and everyone needed a little boozeola retanking, they drove out south to Snappy's Roadhouse. In the graveled lot, not caring to keep it secret at all, a man was beating a woman. She was no lithe doe of a creature, but he was huge and had the bloodlust. Eric uses the word "Neanderthal." They could hear each blow land distinctly, like a live fish being whipped against brick.

Now Eric is big but mild. "I'm not brave, so I must have been drunk," he says. "I stepped on out of the group — we'd been gawking there dumfounded really — and cleared my throat and said 'You shouldn't do that.' He turned around — well, there I was, standing in my vanilla-white stage Stetson, and my bandanna, and fringe, and all — and he snarled 'Who the *hell* are you?' And I snapped back — I don't know where it came from — 'I'm Death! I've dealt out death a hundred times and I'm prepared to deal death a hundred more!'"

At that, the stunned lunk falls to his knees and, in some drunk pathetic display of last-stand anger that already had the soft edge of defeat about it, starts flinging handfuls of gravel and dirt at Eric.

Ever since being told this anecdote, I've carried him — *Neanderthalensis denim* — as a cartoon totem of what I've witnessed dozens of similar times, and seen unsurely peeking out of the pupils in eyes of women and men who are my friends, as out of cave mouths: waiting for night to escape by, waiting for some excuse. I've felt him rise in me and lope across the 60,000 years in seconds, pressing *his* face against the meatside of *my* face, forcing raw chunks of air through my mouth, a perfect fit. And although he's never stepped out of me fully, or out of most of those people I love, I've seen such adrenalin-red contort us sometimes, seen us start to work such bullying over each other. I know he's always asleep back there with one ear cocked — asleep with one hand on his club.

For isn't that the truth of ontogeny's repeating the germinant bullets of fur and eelskin we once were, that are lodged in the psyche, born into us with us? *There,* in the bud — in the gleam of the bud, where gender was undifferentiated — the coward and the aggressor were Siamese pulses, and our hungers were slaked by drinking straight and deep from a runnel of blood. And it's still *here*, a midden buried in the cortex, with its own slithering shadowy life. On nights when we sleep after fighting, I wake and turn to Skyler's turned back. I can feel an anger released through her skin so palpable and steady that I understand it's the radiant half-life of something decaying in us that was whole long before we were fetal.

Meanwhile, Eric's musician friends had alerted Snappy of the bruising taking place in his parking lot. "Boys," said Snappy, "go get him," and out of nowhere two of the house goons filled the night. These guys were Brahman bulls, down to the hump and the dewlap. And they had guns. They needed only to take two token steps in his direction and Neanderthal man, all slobbery now in after-madness, stumbled on back to his van.

You never know, while it's ongoing, what enormous space exists between your perception of action Out There and the action's own needs. I've witnessed this dozens of times in various versions, either sex on either side of it. That rescued woman, saved from maybe a broken jaw, maybe from worse? "You get the fuck out of here, you fucks!" she was shrieking. "You leave my man alone!"

* * * *

Much later, I told Eric's little tale to a lady I know, a poet. "Wow," she responded. "I think I could *really* make use of that in a poem."

2.

This one is turmeric-red: a soldier, in close-up, in 'Nam, in pain we can't imagine except for the size of the scream pushing out of his mouth. This one is a treeline in winter: each pine under its tipi of snow. This one is "avant-garde" collage: bits of headlines, peekaboo snippets of nudie snapshots, torn Old Masters. This one is a treeline in summer: overnight, the catalpas have blossomed in clutches that look like popcorn. This one . . .

—Covers of books of poetry, on sale at the Associated Writing Programs' annual convention. Everybody's here this year, *everybody*. The poet whose first three collections all take place negotiating the scarps of the Rockies, "clambering juts / until we reach the level / sweep of plateau foliage," is here in the penthouse bar negotiating contractual terms for a fourth book. In the panels room, the poet whose "life is dedicated to bringing Women's Struggle to Third World consciousness" is answering questions on how to apply for a reading circuit of Midwest junior colleges: ". . . and will they make me visit composition classes?"

I can't say "something is wrong here." First, I'm here as well. I'm even enjoying myself, an extra-bourbon-over-the-line's-worth. And second, some few of these people are truly doing writing that tallies the double-entry ledger columns of auricle and ventricle exaltingly. Their published work has flowered great rashes of furor or sudden-struck understanding over my ho-hum innards. If this congregation of spiel and shtick with the welcoming marquee in front is part of some field, the ground from which such necessary labor arises, so be it.

But just a bourbon ago it was easy to feel a load less chummy. I *know* these people, and know *of* these people: their days are devoted to teaching poetry, reading poetry, editing poetry journals, mailing out poems of their own to poetry journals, keeping track of poetry grants and contests like inveterate race buffs scanning their sheets for track tips, gossiping poetry, networking poetry, carrying poetry and self-promotional flyers in their attaché cases, playing poetry tennis, organizing poetry lobbying and poetry-for-social-change and a range of poetry therapies, reviewing poetry, scoring poetry points for reviewing poetry, sleeping poetry, and often enough—it will happen in this hotel this evening—sleeping with another poet who's busily sleeping poetry.

Properly or not, by frightening lightninglike blasts or by continuous scratchings of ordinary matches in convention lobbies, poetry conflagrates their lives.

This never appears in the poems themselves. In one, a deep-sienna photograph—now bleached by decades of sun to a marmalade color—shows the poet's grandparents serving a party of gubernatorial hangers-on, and so implicitly asks what small integrities they may have kept for themselves as secret signals traded across the opulent room, while they tended to White Man's business. In another the poet considers cosmology theory while studying the vibrant spirals painted on vases for sale in a Guatemalan village square. In this one, the poet gives voice to the "dead tongues" lolling out of shoes in a Goodwill thrift shop, "those who hobbled, those who sprinted," whose mysterious spirit now sings to us as the night grows permissive, sings "as one scuffed choir."

Would we want it any other way?—a poem about a poet's peddling poems, then peddling more poems. I think not.

But I also wonder what it means, this space between a life's most constant activity and its public expression?

That night in the hotel room, I look through *my* poems: archaeological ruins are being whistled indifferently through, by the wind; and ideas of how much circumstance love may bear, without crumbling, are set against this backdrop of broken-crowned, houndstoothed columns.

The light of a hotel bathroom is surgically stark. Inside my face, another man is stumblingly checking *his* face. I think now he's a third-year welder at Casey J's Assembly Shop, and he's good at his job, and honest with the customers, and he sweats his ass off overtime, sometimes, just to help her pay for the orthodontia work for the seven-year-old who isn't even *his*, although he likes the kid and takes him to the ball games that the church group sponsors on Saturdays. All he knows is he tries hard and then some; *damn* hard. Why did they have to humiliate him that way in the parking lot? Okay, so he was drunk and got a little riled—she'll do that to you, she *likes* to do that to you. But he didn't deserve the way those assholes treated him in front of her—hell, no one deserves being treated like that.

* * * *

"The cave men," Jim tells me, "are standing around as if they're at the bus stop, they're that real. They're carrying hunks of rock that might as well be thermoses." In preparation for doing his new novel, where the ancient powers speak through tribal masks and reconstructed skeletal figures in museum display halls, Jim's been flying from Austin to New York to talk with diorama masters.

"Think of it, Albert: in just a few inches of space, they need to indicate dozens of miles of distance," he says with his hand waving "miles-of-distance-sign" above his plate of hot *cabrito*, and I *do* conjure up some hackneyed sfumato Neanderthal skyline, ruggedly featured and cave-pocked in receding detail.

"All of the mannequins need to be arranged without shadows, or grouped so their shadows don't botch the illusion. That's the art—like *our* art," and he winks. "No matter how shallow *really,* the good ones sustain an illusion of depth."

3.

We could tell it wouldn't work. We were "in love," but knew it wouldn't work. For one thing, Noona was—had been, for three or four years, and only after intense and willful attempts to reconstruct herself in exactly this way—a lesbian. So it was nuts that summer she cheated on her she-spouse with me, giddy with infatuation, sick with guilt, betraying her recent gay-sexual allegiance (that in turn betrayed her earlier heterosexual identity), confused, ecstatic, keeping both Meg and myself on *hold* in the thick June air while she queried the sky with a hundred of the Grand Old Human Questions, testing her gender preference, running from it, enchanted by me, committed to Meg, alive past the brim of each neuron, too high-minded for this low sneaking-around, disgusted, delighted, sleepless, and split at the pit of herself like a room freeze-framed a second after the bomb goes off.

She taught me about containment—she could hold herself-like-a-genie all day inside of herself-like-a-lamp. And a genie has undeniable power. I was teaching her things too, I think, little kinds of zaniness she must have seen as carrying childishness with bravery into an adult life. Our time together, filched and scant, was magic, but we knew it wouldn't work.

When I look back now, what I see are uncountable mornings waiting at 5:00 A.M. in the lot for hospital staff. She walks to her car—the look of pleasure and worn-down hopelessness at seeing me there is so strong it could tumble off her face and crack on the macadam. Then she leans her forehead against the dawn cool of the car, with a weary deliberation, as if the inertness of metal itself might transfer over, and bring her a moment's peace. I have my hands in my pockets, then rest them around her, then back in their pockets . . . there's nothing to say, or do. This lasts about a zillion years, and when I look back now, it's all that happened that summer. By August I'd packed up for Wichita, Kansas.

I don't wish to reveal lots more about it, but this is pertinent: Noona was the daughter of an alcoholic father. So much has been written about the syndromes—like a family of representative stick-figure people: The Syndromes! What I want to see now is that six-year-old girl in her frayed plaid skirt, at hopscotch under the el-train thunder one afternoon in the sticky air of the end of the school year, listening to her friends describe *their* summer plans, and inventing, in her turn, like crazy: they were going to drive to England to visit Walt Disney and the Pope.

Already learning to play the nothing-is-wrong-at-home game. Feeling the plaster rigidify over her face—the cast she wore while waiting for the healing—then *becoming* the face. Already learning to love it.

So, later, she dated the guy who beat her, needing to explain away the delicate Chinese plums of bruise she'd wear to work. She lived with the guy who cheated on her, in front of her, explaining away his "sister's" unexpected overnight visit and then his "cousin's." They needed her, just like the father, and she needed *that*. So Meg was perfect, whose angers and terrors required tender holding. At Meg's insistence, this wasn't any casually revealed lesbian romance. They were "roommates," if the world inquired. No one could be invited over. Noona's parents "would die" if they "knew"; Meg's ditto. Now Noona was able to turn her back on a planet of victimizing men, yet still lead the life of Deep Secret. Safe in the fortress, peering for enemies out of the slot in its door.

And me?—what hidden history did *I* schlep to our few doomed months? I'm not going to say, but I'll tell you this: it was mightily there. In each of us, from a central mulch where the oxygen gets chemically fired onto the red-cell lozenges: it's there. Richard Leakey, in *People of the Lake:* "Beyond thirty-five thousand years ago, there is no more recent sign of the Neanderthal race. They vanished. However, they may not have suffered complete biological oblivion: they may instead have interbred with the mainstream. The genes of Neanderthalers may be surviving in us all today."

The space is the length of light from our skin to the sun. The space is the span of a hand. It can't be calibrated in the usual ruled units. Listen: Noona was a nurse, as her mother had been. "You see it, in front of your nose, but then you snap it closed inside a locket somewhere a solar system away, in your medulla oblongata, or you can't go on." The first time she carried a raw arm "like a baby" from the operating table, and dropped it . . . Listen: that sound.

The camera dollying up to her face, then zooming through the irises: asteroids, intergalactic emptiness, universe dust, and then a tiny white moon with a splatter of fresh blood. Noona isn't her real name — not for an instant — but the arm is real and keeps on falling, the size of a splinter you'd get in your eye, forever.

* * * *

"Go know," my mother always says, then lobs it to her listener with that decades-practiced fatalistic shrug. It means: just *try* to make sense of a world defined by what's obscure and ephemeral. Fight City Hall. Count angels on a pinhead.

. . . now he's picking up the kid with his mouthful of hardware from the Jew orthodontist's, *whoopsie,* twirling him up in the air with that goony metal-plated smile he gets, and then they're off with a thermos of some orangeade pee, to watch their team The Saints beat the holy crap out of the Pillars of Fire, and something — *something,* a petal of butteriness, you might say loving-kindness — opens up in his gut when the kid is around, so he wants to kiss the gimp pop vendor, tell him here's a twenty, keep the change . . .

On one page, Leakey evokes "the Neanderthal race, a stocky, beetle-browed people." In the life-size diorama Jim saw, "They're staring out of some muttering, conspiratorial huddle, you know, with that truculent jaw-set of neighborhood thugs." As he chews this mouthful, he's cubing his face, in imitation. Slobbers. But Leakey says also, of ritual burial: "Ironically, one of the earliest and least equivocal instances of this moving behavior is at a Neanderthal site in the Zagros Mountains. There, in the Shanidor Cave, a man was laid to rest on a bed of flowers more than sixty thousand years ago."

Hear the whistle of wind through that number.

Go know.

4.

There's something plainspoken and forthright to the idea of nudism—wearing only yourself for the world, no intervening arrangements. If you're bruised, that sickly mustard carnation shows. If the wind flicks your nipples, they're fissured. It would seem that here, at least, we're undone layers closer to an openness.

But notice, I said "the *idea* of nudism." Look at those well-known photographs by Diane Arbus, taken at Jersey and Pennsylvania nudist camps over a five-year period starting in 1962: the couple in the woods, who have achieved some station halfway between a medieval oil of Adam and Eve, and a peeper's candid snapshot; or the fat, the simply *fat,* family whose picnic looks like a beaching of sea cows; yes, or the platinum housewife in her swan sunglasses. "They run the whole social gamut," Arbus said, "from people in tents to people in mansions almost."

And she said that after a while she "began to wonder about nudist camps. . . . There'd be an empty pop bottle or rusty bobby pin—the lake bottom oozes in a particularly nasty way and the outhouse smells, the woods look mangy." Now this is strangely finicky perturbation from someone who reveled in her cast of 42nd Street subjects shuffling their way at 3:00 A.M. through the alleycat shit and used needles: gaudy ostrich-plumed dwarf pimps, their stables of rouged-up blowjob peddlers, lip-picking mumblers, gutter scavengers, self-proclaimed princes in exile, addict pickpockets, guys who'll pay you to kick them, *hard* . . . It doesn't exactly make a "rusty bobby pin" look outrageous.

But she'd *expect* the 42nd Street grunge. What I suspect Arbus was registering is a disappointment in how the average nudist colony falls off from a preconceived ideal. It's this space between the absolute and the actual, growing increasingly moldy and dreck-bestrewn, that has her upset. This space can't be computed by any objectively rendered scale, but my grandparents traveled it one afternoon as the ferry rounded Liberty, her torch held toward the heavens, then started choppily closing in on the din and muck of ghetto New York at the turn of the century. Such babel-array of pidginspeaks. Such streetcar-clanging hell nights.

And such possibility. Here, through this space, a charge builds up — the multi-cultural *salsa-&-gefilte* power of immigrants — that begins dirt-poor and ends a generation later with manicured lawns, that huddles around a trash-barrel fire in winter, sleeps, and suffers, then wakes with the grandson replacing a furnace filter and clomping back up to the TV den. Between, a lot of love gets smuggled from one sad time to another. And maybe some brains get bashed in — go know. This isn't space that exists in topography. Astronomy's "red shift" calculations can't chart such direction and speed. I'll say this: we share 99.9 percent of our genes with Neanderthal man and woman. When we wake up as ourselves, it's with one-tenth of one percent of genetic difference turning our engines over, blinking in the new day's sunlight, marveling at the purr. Go measure. Angels on a pinhead.

When my grandfather woke with his arm around Nettie, his other arm was crushed by one of the fourteen lowlife huckster Jews they shared their first week's lodgings with. Their world was filth and raw energy, the alley song of the scissors-grinder man, the glow of Sabbath candles doubled by a rat's eyes, scams and shameless flimflam, prayer shawls and finger-sized streetfight knives, the militant suffragette picketers on their feet and the whores on their asses, steaming horse dung on the winter street and a baby found frozen to the light pole so its belly tore off when they moved it, slitting chickens open, slitting holes for buttons, and the irrepressible beauty of a full moon whether or not the bars of the fire escape presented her in prisoner's stripes. He woke, it was night, with fourteen other people around; but he kissed her.

I think Arbus would have snapped it all with relish. Someone did, on occasion. Just like that black poet ransacking family attic albums for material — I have photographs, or retrospective half-imagined photographs, glazed over by a long marinade of tough going.

I wake, I see Skyler's awake. Whatever we were angry about the day before, I see that sleep has milled it down to the lightest-weight flyaway chaff. Somewhere in the cave-back of our dreams, survival was being fought out: a matter of clubs. We're *here* now, though, just live skins needing stroking.

We pass our hands over each other like metal detectors, looking to heal each other, maybe partially *of* each other, searching to ease the last scraplet of shrapnel out.

* * * *

There's a standard magazine gag we've all seen: on a shoreline, a middle-aged male nudist passes a nubile young nudist woman. And in the thought-balloon over his head, risen like a cloud from his secretmost fantasy deeps, he pictures her: *clothed.*

And so we see that no situation, no matter how all-revealing, obviates our having some life concealed. If there's anything that saves these two from being so cartoony they'd blow off the page at a breath—if anything carries them one-tenth of one percent toward being human at all—it's the rise of that private vision.

5.

In *A Little Book on the Human Shadow,* Robert Bly writes, "I think one could say that most Puritans did not distinguish darkness from Satan," and that, to this day, "our culture teaches us from early infancy to split and polarize dark and light. . . . Behind us we have an invisible bag, and the part of us our parents don't like, we, to keep our parents' love, put in the bag." We do the same for teachers, peer groups, lovers, and careers. Sexuality, spontaneity, anger, jealousy, men their feminine selves, and women their male beings, "a desire to kill animals and smear their blood on our faces, a desire to get away from all profane life and live religiously"—these are the kinds of energies "preserved from our mammal inheritance" and "our 5,000 years of tribal life" that we stuff, early on, in the bag: "and we spend the rest of our lives trying to get them out again."

Bly is eager to emphasize that this interior darkness is not evil: "the shadow energies seem to be a part of the human psyche, and . . . become destructive only when they are ignored." He draws the metaphor of Dr. Jekyll's Hyde-self, i.e., hidden self, that "feels rage from centuries of suppression," running fatally amok.

What he suggests (and he sketchily starts to get prescriptive in this) is "honoring the shadow": "If we don't live our animal side or our sexual side, that means we don't *honor* those parts. If we have anger and do not make proper clothing for it . . . that means we are failing to honor our anger."

Two hundred years earlier, Blake wrote, "He who desires but acts not, breeds pestilence." And, "The lust of the goat is the bounty of God. The wrath of the lion is the wisdom of God. The nakedness of woman is the work of God."

The space in us where shadow theater stages its productions can't be walked in a day or dreamed in a night — "near as a grosbeak, far as Orion," says the poet Antler.

We're the audience. We're the featured stars.

* * * *

Sometimes, researching the records, we could think that every American town in the decades clustered around 1900 had its pair of "spinster librarians" living in a frame house at the town edge, liked by everyone although pitied as well. Two figures admitted completely and even warmly into community life although rarely invited into people's drawing rooms, they were "so sweet," "yet reclusive," and "uncommonly sisterly towards one another in those small gestures of deference which betoken a large understanding": "though it was many the June-struck couple who drifted apart, these two gray ladies, as dependable as the cycling of seasons, lasted with whatever their contentment was, through the winter of life." What extra pleasure attached to their sacrosanctdom? what unbearable isolation?

And across town, when his wife attended the charity meet, then didn't Mr. Whistler the banker stroke her petticoats, languidly stroking himself, and living in some enormously silky heaven that folded for propriety's sake to fit in his brain's electrical wiring? Yes. And at the edge of town, the spinster Hawkins is waiting up for the spinster Shea, who rode to church to organize the charity meet, and she'll return with wicked gossip on everyone, and share it as the bun unpins and her tresses fall like a silver fox stole to her shoulders . . .

Noona, there was always the space a leaf falls through, between us. I don't think that Meg's the answer for you, but some lady ought to be, some day. Maybe you'll read this. Then you'll understand it's a long-delayed letter, written to wish *good luck,* the words I had on my tongue that last afternoon, but its light was too fierce and they crawled back down to curl up in a dark nest of organs.

* * * *

There are spaces; and under them, spaces. So the poet raised by two professor-parents is revising a poem on feral children supposedly raised by wolves. And who am I to say an equal gap doesn't exist between this plane of very visible, reportable activity, and some level of cellular urgency?—a gap across which charge accrues, and a solitary howling is heard. A leaf falls, hitting ground; and over time, over units of worm and of rain, falls through the ground. These are the lessons of physics. Spaces are composed of more spaces. Spaces composed of similar spaces can love and hurt each other, as if they were solid.

* * * *

"In *santeria* religion," Jim says, "they seance regularly with the dead. I was invited: all these chicken bones still glistening, and a perfectly credible voice, I guess we'd say 'emanating,' from out of the woman in charge." It's for his novel. "What I want is that same Ancestral Voice conducted up the bodies in the planet, like through circuitry, and sounding out of cowrie-shell ritual masks in the museum corners. And something in your own marrow wants to talk back. Neat, huh?"

Go know.

And the Wild Boy of Aveyron, and Wild Peter of Hanover, and the Lithuanian Bear-Boy. Kamala, eight, and Amala, one-and-a-half, were reportedly found on all fours "among wolf cubs in a giant abandoned anthill on the outskirts of a village in India" seventy years ago. For food, they killed small chickens, eating them raw. "Amala died within a year, but Kamala, who lived to be eighteen, learned to walk, wear clothing, and speak a few words." What a cosmos she traveled every day just to reach the near wall of the courtyard!

* * * *

One night Sarah, Eric, Skyler, and I quick-hit a neighborhood carnival, the gypsy kind that sets up in a mall lot and is gone next week. It was late. I know the ride operators looked surly and bored. Whatever the reason, those thousand hours we jolted around the tilt-a-whirl were *most* unpleasant. We spent the rest of the night on our backs, recuperating, calming our semicircular canals' upheaving fluids. I remember repeating, over and over, the phrase that Eric had first used on the seedy little midway, to persuade me as we promenaded past the thing: "a really *classic* carnival ride."

What made it worse was, we'd eaten at Snappy's. Snappy himself was there, as always, wearing his yoke-front cowboy shirt and el cheapo linoleum-looking toupee. As always, he was receiving or handing over to someone a pile of folded money about as thick as a Victorian novel. And yes, as always, the grease-scummed food was just one-*n*th of a floury dollop away from being completely indigestible.

But everybody knows that Snappy's restaurant, if "restaurant" isn't overglorification, exists up front to launder the bigtime cash flow generated in the compound out back, in a huge L-shaped and windowless building. Gambling. Black market cameras and watches. "Once I walked into the annex and a sixteen-year-old girl was cavorting buck-nekkid on the tables," Eric says. "I got me some looks said I wasn't invited."

Snappy gets driven around in his own stretch limo, the one with longhorns mounted for the hood ornament. Snappy clicks his fingers and gun-toting hooligans beam out of the floor. Snappy stars in hundreds of photographs covering not only the walls but the *ceiling:* shaking the councilman's hand, wearing his fraternal organization cowl and corsage-like medals, visiting the orphans' home with a sackload of goodies, fishing with the missus. Other photographs are warmly inscribed: ventriloquists, magicians, local politicians, old-time country fiddler groups, a number of tassel-tittied strippers, rodeo cowboys, civic leagues.

I wouldn't want to start counting the precariously balanced team of Snappies inside this man.

But I would like, one time, to tour the back compound; to casually walk up to the eight-foot plaster horseshoe framing its single entrance; to cover the distance as he does daily, dozens of times, in just a few steps, to walk from the whirr of the world's common traffic, the litter a breeze skitters under my feet, then my hand on the doorknob in shadow.

* * * *

There are many books I've brought back from the convention. Poetry poetry poetry.

Here, the cover of this one is the Earth itself in geode-like cross-section, so all of the layers of grandparents, buried terraces, potsherds, carnelian, oil, and coal are shown like striation in cuts of meat, and then on down to the turbulent, almost unthinkably inhuman, magma heart.

On the surface, a marble temple with delicate fluted columns appears to look up toward the stars.

Colophon

A Sympathy of Souls was designed by Allan Kornblum, at Coffee House Press, using the Xerox Ventura Publisher program on a Terrapin 386sx computer. The compugraphic version of Baskerville type was generated by Stanton Publication Services, Minneapolis, Minnesota. This book was printed on acid-free paper, and the pages were smyth-sewn for added durability. The book was printed and bound by McNaughton & Gunn, Ann Arbor, Michigan.